THE WHEELCHAIR GOES EAST

Hong Kong, Macau and Mainland China: May 2018

Mike Fox

The Wheelchair Goes East
Copyright © 2021 by Mike Fox

Library of Congress Control Number: 2020923373
ISBN-13: Paperback: 978-1-64749-130-7
            E-pub: 978-1-64749-294-6

Although every precaution has been taken to verify the accuracy of the information contained herein, the author and publisher assume no responsibility for any errors or omissions.No liability is assumed for damages that may result from the use of information contained within.

Printed in the United States of America

GoToPublish LLC
1-888-337-1724
www.gotopublish.com
info@gotopublish.com

Contents

OUR TRAVELS IN CHINA

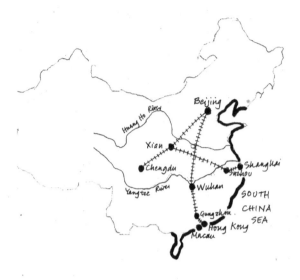

Other books by Mike Fox

Travelling by Road, Rail, Sea, Air (and Wheelchair) in North America

Vamos a Brasil! Recollections of a Volunteer Attempting to Teach English in Brazil

The Pivo Tour of Slovakia: Memoirs of an Anglo-Slovak student exchange – The observations of an outsider

The Italian Therapy Job: A Travel Diary

Introduction

This is the story of an adventure undertaken by my wife Sylvia and me, in which we covered vast distances overland across China, mainly by train; we only resorted to air travel at the start and close of our Odyssey. I am just old, but reasonably mobile, I think, for my age. My wife, Sylvia, however, has Parkinson's disease, compounded by being in need of a knee replacement operation in May 2018 (which tuned out to be a failure but that's a story for another time) and which left her in need of a wheelchair for most of her travelling. But Sylvia is a fighter and was certainly up for the experience of seeing such an interesting country.

Our travel story is complicated but also enriched by the people we met on our way, some of whom became our travel companions. The dramatis personae of our journey of exploration include our elder son, Nathan, who is based in Macau for his work and his partner Melodie, both of whom became our near-constant companions for a sizeable chunk of the itinerary (from Macau to Beijing and on to Xian); we couldn't have asked for more from them. But in Beijing, one of our former students, Zhiping, who has stayed with us on several occasions back home in the UK, met us along with her husband, Lu Yang, and basically took a week off work to show us many sides of her city where they now live.

We were also privileged to contact friends from years gone by in Macau and Hong Kong and share time and food together in convivial surroundings. We also met, for the first time, a delightful Chinese young lady, Jessica, on a boat in Shanghai, and we now count her as one of our friends. In between our 'solo' travels, we linked up with travel guides from the company *Wendy Woo*. Every one of the guides was friendly, helpful, knowledgeable and experienced in catering for disabled people. We would not hesitate to use them again.

As if all this was not enough, we experienced many random acts of kindness shown to us by both the people we met and on occasions, from people in the street, which made us feel quite special. These included an old lady in Chengdu, walking along the street, who welcomed us to her city; a lady who asked us for a selfie with her in the Summer Palace; people offering to help us with our wheelchair when the going seemed to be challenging; guards on the Great Wall who cheered Sylvia when she heroically scaled the steps onto the parapet – and a host of characters who wanted to talk and tried their best to be helpful in various situations.

Coming away from China, we feel we have made new friendships and cemented existing ones. We experienced kindness everywhere. We also experienced a country on the move, with an amazingly impressive railway system, not to mention dynamic urban planning, as well as areas and landscapes of great beauty.

I indulged in one of my favourite activities – riding trains – and some of them were sleek, fast, comfortable, convenient and punctual. I gather that since we were in China, a new, high-speed railway line has been opened between Beijing and Hong Kong; so, we rode in a train that is now history, but none the less interesting for that.

And of course, we aim to return some day.

Mike Fox

Tram congestion, in Hong Kong

A Long Journey

Chaos reigns at home as the time for our taxi to the station draws near. There is the big (and I mean really big) case to finish packing and Sylvia is still looking for her toothbrush. But our taxi driver, who arrives on time, is friendly and says that our journey to China has made him happy. I think he is happy in the sense of being happy for us, as opposed to wishing to get rid of us. He seems genuinely excited by our holiday.

A young woman on the station platform asks if she can help with our cases; she is about to sit her finals exams in psychology at Plymouth University and her thesis topic is memory and motor skills, at which point I decide not to ask any further questions.

Despite a dire weather forecast, the sun comes out to play, and the countryside, especially in Somerset and Wiltshire, is looking resplendent in the light and shadows. The train passes through Castle Carey, where the station is surrounded by fields – it seems to have 'lost' its town, with agricultural barns seemingly outnumbering the houses.

Sylvia manages to do my trick and flood our complimentary copy of the Times newspaper with sparkling water, but our amiable Polish train hostess sees the funny side and replaces it with a pristine copy. The glorious weather is too good to last, and the train slows down in the rain through grey west London suburbs.

At the baggage check-in at Heathrow Airport, I'm informed by the official that our really big case weighs in at 22.7 kilos, which she says is right on the limit. Observing the people around us at the departure lounge, it seems to me that there is a pattern of younger, mainly Chinese ladies carrying lightweight bags, followed by their husbands, partners, boyfriends (even fathers) carrying heavy loads of merchandise. The London shopping scene must still be doing well.

Our Jamaican wheelchair pusher at the airport doesn't stop chatting for the duration of the push. She gets seriously misled over our gate location and lets the airport management staff know about it. At one point she adjusts my backpack and I sense someone well into sport; and true enough, she says that she was a basketball coach. It's interesting that several staff members compliment her on her stylish clothing. *"I normally wear purple, but today it's grey, and my mates seem to like it,"* she says. Yes, she does look good in grey.

We are on board the British Airways Boeing A380 Airbus a good 15 minutes before take-off. Sylvia has a window seat with a great view of the aircraft wing. In the end our take-off is late, at ten past seven in the evening, in the late sunshine. The Shard, Europe's tallest building, stands out magnificently in the distance.

On the flight I listen to some melodic, surreal instrumental music by Nils Frahn, followed by a relaxing Coldplay concert. I put the flight map on and drift into something approaching sleep as we fly over vast swathes of the Russian Federation.

Sylvia struggles to get to and from the toilet at around midnight, but the stewards make us hot drinks and even offer alternative seats if we wish.

Thursday 3 May

Hong Kong Revisited

At some time in the small hours, I listen to great songs from Cuba and Senegal, including music from Baaba Maal and Ruben Gonzalez. I am pretty tired by seven in the morning and I note the temperature is registering at 30°C as we touch down at Hong Kong airport at one thirty in the afternoon.

Times Square, near our hotel

Fortunately our pre-booked taxi driver arrives quickly with our names on a card; now we know what it feels like to be a VIP! As we are driven in towards the centre, the impression of Hong Kong as a dynamic city and sea port has not diminished over the years. Some of the container terminals we can see are immense, and there are ships in the harbour, between the islands and out in the ocean as far as the eye can see. The visual impact of the cranes, ships, tug boats and other marine vessels is only matched by the profusion of high-rise flats and tall commercial buildings and the vibrant, pulsating atmosphere of the place.

Despite its reputation as a city in perpetual gridlock, the traffic in the middle of the day here in Hong Kong is running smoothly. It certainly is as we drive along the coastal strip of the island of Lantau and cross over the bridge into Kowloon on the Hong Kong mainland. When we first visited Hong Kong in 1989, Lantau was a rural island with virtually no traffic. The new airport has changed all that, although the western, most rural end has been largely protected from development. Driving eastwards towards Kowloon, there are now serried ranks of tall apartment blocks looking down on the new rail link connecting the airport with downtown Hong Kong. In the vicinity of these high-rise buildings, the railway passes under a concrete shelter. If not to protect the railway from snow, I wonder what is the purpose of the shelters; maybe from anything 'dropped' from a flat 20 storeys above? Or perhaps from the ravages of a typhoon?

Peak Tram

A misty view of Hong Kong from the Peak

I revise my initial view on congestion in Hong Kong once we cross the bridge into Kowloon where there is slow moving traffic everywhere. By the time we have driven through the tunnel and entered Hong Kong Island we are virtually in gridlock, and the taxi driver's estimation of one hour from the airport to the hotel proves to be accurate. We pass through a concrete, glass and steel forest of skyscrapers at a very slow speed.

We are deposited at the right hotel, the Holiday Inn in Causeway Bay after my initial doubts. The hotel reception staff reassuringly say they are expecting us and they pass me an envelope containing our train tickets from Hong Kong to Beijing, which we will use next Monday. We are escorted by friendly and helpful staff to a wheelchair friendly bedroom, which is pleasant and spacious. The shower is good, although as a non-disabled person, I have to bend down to get beneath the shower head, and in this case, Sylvia has the last laugh.

In the early evening we eat at a small restaurant next door to the hotel reception. I avoid the edible frog and rabbit's claws, play a straight bat and opt for noodles, beef and green vegetables. It tastes good and I even enjoy a cup of China tea which is refilled by the waiters at least twice.

We also notice that there are restaurants in the hotel block all the way up to the sixth floor, so whatever happens tomorrow we are not going to starve in Hong Kong.

Our final activity of the day is a walk/push around the neighbourhood, where our hotel is one block away from Times Square, at around nine o'clock. We do this, despite the fact that it is pouring with rain - but at least in Hong Kong the rain isn't cold! (And it makes for atmospheric photographs.) There is no shortage of people on the move, as the area around the hotel is full of restaurants, not to mention late night shopping and an interesting concentration of Thai massage parlours. The only negative aspect is the dearth of wheelchair-friendly crossing points across the roads.

And of course it is early to bed.

Heavy rain in Causeway Bay, Hong Kong, on our first night

The Peak and Old Friends

We take the lift down to breakfast. On the way, we pass one lift with a sign which says what is on the six floors below, for example, restaurants, conference rooms, etc., and at the end of the list, the sign concludes by saying *"They are not accessible from this floor"*!

After waiting in a short queue, we hand over our breakfast coupons before entering a hive of activity, which strikes me as something akin to a ship's galley. There are a lot of people moving around in a confined space, with some polite jostling. One of the breakfast staff accidentally bumps into me and he is quick to apologise. He then asks me if I want coffee and crème and says he will bring it to my table. One of the staff tries to teach me 'welcome' in Cantonese, but my attempts to say it only result in mirth.

Back in our hotel room, the phone rings. It is Liz, whom we last saw in 1989 when she and her partner Josh spent Christmas with us in England. They now live in the New Territories, and we agree to meet up in the Xin Dao Ji Chinese restaurant on the second floor of our building. Liz says they have lived in Hong Kong since 1997, but these days they never go to Hong Kong Island – *"It's where all the kids go on a Saturday night"*, she explains. They say they will bring another friend of ours, Lai, with them, whom we also last met in 1989 in the UK, when he was an engineer based in Woking, Surrey.

I have clear memories of when I took Liz, Josh, Lai and another Chinese friend Chris, to the Dartmoor National Park, near where we live in the UK, in December of that year. We had just scaled Hay Tor, one of our favourite granite peaks for a half an hour's stroll, and sometime after we set off through the National Park back to our home, I still remember Liz telling the Chinese men off for falling asleep in the back of our car – *"Mike's showing you all this beautiful scenery and all you can do is sleep!"*

Late in the morning, we take a taxi to the Peak Tram, something we have experienced several times before but an activity we never tire of doing. Sylvia gets priority boarding, along with her wheelchair, and I tag along, taking advantage of Sylvia's disability. We do this to the tune of public announcements every few minutes in Cantonese, Mandarin and English, telling people to move onto the tram in an orderly fashion and then thanking everyone for their cooperation.

A Spanish lady sits next to us in the tram, whilst her daughter stands. Her daughter is working in Shanghai. The lady tells us that most of her daughter's friends despair of the place after a few years, but two years into her stay her daughter is still enjoying the experience, but she is upset about the prospect of having to move to London with her insurance job. She is pleased when I tell her that I am happy banking with Santander, especially as she comes from Bilbao, which isn't too far away from the Santander headquarters along the northern Spanish coast.

The dark red, two-coach tram looks resplendently Victorian as it trundles quite noisily up the steep track towards the Peak. The tower blocks to our right look like exaggerated versions of the Leaning Tower of Pisa. The tram makes it to the Peak Visitor Centre and disgorges us into a bland mass of concrete and glass. We manage to get special assistance to access the viewing platform at a higher level. The magnificent harbour, however, looks grey and subdued in the rain and slight mist and in these conditions, my photographs are not going to turn out to be brilliant.

We make our way from the Peak Visitor Centre along a footpath which largely keeps to the same contour and is quite wheelchair friendly. At this relatively high altitude, we can feel the cool, fresh air and the sound of birdsong. A kind lady from London comes over and offers to take a photograph of us, which is a sweet gesture. We also get chatting to a local artist who is selling his pictures and he gives me a special discount price for five paintings, together with a sapphire charm for Sylvia and a Man Utd keyring for me, saying: "*We are in the Cup Final, facing the common enemy!*"

Close to the Visitor Centre, we come across an attractive, traditionally designed stone building by the name of the Peak Lookout Restaurant. It has leafy gardens overlooking the sea. Although the food is not cheap, we enjoy superb smoked salmon and tropical fruit juice in congenial surroundings. As we leave, our waiter runs after us to hand me my glasses, which I have left on the table; stupid boy that I am!

At the Peak Visitor Centre, we are again given special assistance to get to the tram. Our attendant has to leave us for a moment and we wait for his return. At this point, a group of tourists from Mainland China completely block our path, which initially isn't a problem, as we are stationary, awaiting the return of the attendant. The leader of this group shouts something in Mandarin (I catch the words "xie xie" (thankyou) at the end of his sentence) and the group move nearer to us, at which point one of the group tries to push me and Sylvia in the wheelchair out of the way. I stand my ground and resist. Our attendant returns, quickly sees what is going on, moves towards the Chinese group and shouts at them, at which point they do get out of the way, allowing us to pass through them. An amusing little incident methinks. I wonder what agendas are being played out, with Sylvia and I as pawns in a bigger picture.

The track seems even steeper as the tram trundles down the hill towards the Mid-Levels area of Hong Kong Island. The spectacular vistas are interrupted by close-up views of massive concrete retaining walls.

At the base of the tram route, we catch a taxi back to our hotel with no trouble, and our folding wheelchair just fits into the boot; a conventional wheelchair would not have made it. Like many taxi drivers out here, he pushes into gaps in the traffic where he has no right to go, and gets the sounding of horns from other drivers to thank him for his efforts!

After chilling out for a couple of hours in our hotel, we wander down to the reception. By perfect synchronisation, our friends Josh and Liz approach us from the top of the entrance escalator and Lai joins us from the hotel lounge – our first meeting since December 1989, half a lifetime ago.

We have booked a table for five at the Xin Dao Ji restaurant, and we take our places. As we haven't seen each other for so long, there's a lot to talk about. But first, Liz gets her partner Josh to order a suitable meal that we can all share. He succeeds admirably. The China tea that comes with the meal is poured as refills into our cups continuously throughout the evening.

Liz is a linguist and works at one of the universities in Hong Kong several days a week. At present she is busy marking examination papers. Lai is still working as a civil engineer and he has just finished a major new road project. He worked at one time for a major transportation engineering consultancy in the south-east of England. But a new opportunity may soon be opening up for him in Vancouver. Liz's partner Josh is still working as an engineer, also for the public sector, but says he is running down towards retirement; I'm not sure Liz believes him.

Our conversation over the next few hours ranges over Australian politics and planning issues – Liz still owns a property in Sydney and travels there several times a year – to places where we have visited, to Brexit (why should Australians want to increase their trade with the UK? Liz argues), to the ageing process and understanding Parkinson's disease. Liz wants to know exactly where in the Japanese island of Hokkaido one of my nephews co-owns a property, and the part of inner Sydney that was home to my brother Andrew and his family before they moved to Warangara on the northern outskirts of the conurbation. So I have been set my homework!

Liz talks about the difficulty of learning Chinese characters for westerners. Lai confirms he is a workaholic, but he looks good on it. Liz says she cannot understand how, in my job, I can make planning decisions without referring them to a board. "*Is the door not open to corruption?*" she asks. I attempt to explain. Sylvia talks about her love of music and how she still plays the piano after the onset of Parkinson's disease, although she has felt it right to resign from the church music team.

We give an invitation to Lai to visit us if his planned route from Hong Kong to Vancouver happens to pass through the UK. And of course, Josh and Liz can come over and see us any time, and we tell them that our current home is even more spacious than the one they spent Christmas with us in 1989. Liz recalls both the wonders and the 'street horror' of her holiday in India, and I am now not so sure it would be a good idea to take Sylvia there. Sylvia still seems keen enough, though.

It's nearly ten at night by the time we part company in the hotel reception area. Liz and Josh have an hour's journey ahead of them as they vanish down the escalator and head for their home in the New Territories; Lai has an easier journey as he now lives on Hong Kong Island. Sylvia makes it back to our room using only her walking stick, but she's tired. It's lights out at midnight.

Saturday 5 May

Meeting Melodie in Macau

It's a difficult start to the day; perhaps jet lag is catching up with us (in fact, our son Nathan, whom we are travelling to Macau to meet, sent us a text last night asking if I was struggling with jet lag). It's another crowded breakfast in our hotel, with little personal space to hand. My breakfast worker friend from yesterday approaches me and asks what I am looking for. I say *"croissants"* – and he fetches some from a not very obvious place and gives me three! At the end of our breakfast I find him, shake his hand, thank him for his help and then he says he hopes to see me again. You never know.

We book onto a jetfoil vessel for the hour's journey across the mouth (or is it mouths?) of the Pearl River Delta, and we sit in a lounge at the front of the vessel; drinks and a chicken meal are complimentary. Looking across from our fast boat to the mainland, what is new this time is the 34-mile long bridge which connects Macau to Hong Kong via at least one community in Mainland China, and which should be open to traffic in a few months' time.

But no one can tell me whether you will drive across the bridge on the left or on the right! In fact, the bridge will only extend as far as Tuen Mun New Town in the New Territories, so the ferry will remain competitive for journeys into downtown Hong Kong. The new bridge is at its most prominent where it spans the main distributary of the Pearl River, looking wafer thin on the far right.

I have also forgotten how many small, rocky and forested islands there are between Hong Kong and Macau.

Peak Lookout Restaurant

Central Square, Coloane

We sail into Macau harbour under the elegant Taipa Bridge. The skyline of the former Portuguese colony is dominated by the high-rise casino blocks, which have sprung up everywhere. Macau is now the Las Vegas of the Orient, with around 20 casinos already operational, and a lot of Chinese to enjoy them. The other new feature to emerge is the light rail system, much of which is elevated, like the Bangkok sky train. It is not yet operational, although its visual impact has already made itself felt.

Our vessel docks alongside a dozen or so other sleek, turbo-propelled sea craft, which in their bright colours make quite an impressive sight. Friendly officials direct us in quite hot temperatures (mid 30's C) to the free shuttle service to our hotel, another in the Holiday Inn chain. This hotel is situated in the giant new Cotai Centre, replete with a number of gambling halls, cafes, restaurants and retail units. A Korean family takes an interest in the challenge I am facing in pushing Sylvia in her wheelchair, plus two main cases and two backpacks. In fact this wonderful family takes over proceedings in quasi-military style. I shake their hands warmly at the Holiday Inn check-in desk to thank them for their helpfulness.

We arrive in our palatial hotel room at around four-thirty in the afternoon. Sylvia revives when she reads the breakfast menu, which comes across as altogether more sophisticated than its counterpart in its sister hotel in Hong Kong, where we have breakfasted over the last two mornings.

Our lovable host   Nathan, Mike, Sylvia and Melodie in Coloane

Just before six o'clock there is a ring on our doorbell. It's Nathan, together with his girlfriend, Melodie. It's our first proper meeting with Melodie apart from the brief chats we have had on Skype when we have got through to Nathan. Any worries we may have had as how to make our introductions evaporate when Melodie gives both Sylvia and I a warm hug – plus a smart carrier bag containing sweets, dried fruit and one or two mementoes from her native Philippines. So now we have a new friend and lots of provisions for our long train journey to Beijing on Monday.

Nathan and Melodie take us out to a Portuguese restaurant in the southern enclave of Coloane. Our taxi drops us off in one of the most traditional parts of Macau, which is well endowed with old buildings, squares and some pedestrian areas, including a labyrinthine network of narrow streets which have relatively little traffic. Old, gnarled trees, many of which seem to have forgotten how to grow vertically, divide into a myriad of improbable angles, reminding me of the baobab trees on the Kenyan grasslands. The gas lamps add to the atmosphere and there is an absence of very tall modern buildings in this neighbourhood. Arguably this, one of the most Portuguese parts of Macau, still retains a semi-rural, laid back feel.

The main square focuses on the Portuguese colonial church of St Francis where in 1989, on our first visit to Macau, the priest of this church, an Italian man then in his eighties, gave each of our children a toy car. But what they remember most is the priest switching on a set of lights which illuminated an array of display cases in which were reposed the bones of Catholic missionaries, including those of Francis Xavier, the founder of the Jesuit Movement.

The old part of Coloane nestles alongside a distributary of the Pearl River, with Mainland China on the opposite bank. Or maybe not Mainland China any more, as it appears that the Chinese authorities have given the land we can see for Macau to administer. A new road tunnel enables access to recently constructed developments on the 'China side', including the Macau University campus and an amusement park. This area has changed out of all recognition since we first came here in 1989, when at night there was hardly a light to be seen in the darkness from the few scattered buildings at that time. As we look across the river, the sky is further illuminated by fireworks and a laser show.

Pearl River, Macau

Historic Coloane

Our restaurant, situated just off a pedestrian square, specialises in Portuguese cuisine. The owner, an elderly gentleman, enjoys the outside equivalent of 'working the room', engaging everyone at the dining tables in conversation. Nathan says he understands every third word of his Cantonese. The gentleman insists on giving us whisky and I haven't the heart to turn him down. He even poses for a photograph and then takes a picture of the four of us. Later, as we walk away from our table after our meal, we see him singing a folk song to another group of diners.

We walk along the river bank, with Nathan and Melodie helping me out with pushing Sylvia's wheelchair. We pass a couple of fishermen who are throwing their lines beyond the mud and into the dark waters of the Pearl River. A few people stand around chatting. There are almost no cars, although the area seems to be well served by buses.

A short timber pier protrudes into the river. We stroll onto it and take in the peaceful atmosphere of Coloane, the quiet Portuguese colonial backwater behind us and the louder and brighter new development on the China side ahead of us.

At 8:30 we stop for a coffee in a local café. We are the only people in the place. It's a pleasant, dry evening, around 24° C, with a slight breeze. It's a very pleasant atmosphere for a stroll.

Our taxi collects us from Coloane and 20 minutes later we are back at the Holiday Inn. We give Nathan and Melodie a day off and we will book tickets for the 10:45 ferry on Monday morning to Kowloon, in time to catch our train to Beijing.

Times Square, Hong Kong

Sunday 6 May

Meeting up with more 'Old Friends'

The biggest challenge this morning is to find the restaurant in the entertainment/ retail/restaurant/hotel complex that goes by the name of Cotai Central. Cotai takes its name from the massive land reclamation scheme which joins the islands of Coloane and Taipa, which were the only two islands in the former Portuguese colony of Macau, compared with over two hundred islands which make up part of Hong Kong.

Sylvia and I walk through the Cotai Central complex, past Rolex, Gucci and other international brand retail outlets, to the Yum Cha restaurant, where we hand in our breakfast coupons. Unlike the 'galley melee' of yesterday, this is altogether a more refined affair. We are directed to a table where we are invited to tick a number of boxes on a dim sum card. But I still can't abide congee and the coffee is very strong. I may break with tradition and opt for China tea tomorrow. Orange juice is not an option to be ticked but I ask for it anyway, and complimentary orange juices are delivered to our table.

There are almost no other non-Chinese in the restaurant. A Hong Kong resident helps Sylvia into her wheelchair when we have finished our breakfast, which is a nice gesture. Sylvia didn't get much sleep last night, so she elects to lie in for a few hours when we return to our room.

I am, however, ready to explore and I leave the air conditioned Cotai Central complex and head out into a clear and sunny day, in the lower 30s°C. I walk past one ostentatious recreation of a world famous landmark after another. These include a plagiarised St Mark's Tower at the Venetian complex, a reduced version of the Eiffel Tower at the Parisian, and a huge statue of a man leaping into the air at The Studio.

The area seems to be especially popular with Arab women, some of whom with almost complete body covering are taking photographs of each other. I also spot separate groups of Arab men but it seems in the Cotai Central area at least, neither the twain shall meet.

Each access to a gambling palace or retail centre has a guy holding back pedestrians to allow cars to pass; pedestrians are definitely further down the pecking order. The ultimate example which seems to say it all is a coach not slowing down and sounding its horn aggressively to scatter pedestrians, many of whom are already more than half way across the access road. The letters at the back of the offending coach – FOOK U – seem to perfectly encapsulate the driver's attitude to any pedestrians who dare to get in his way.

Some of the messages in English on the T-shirts seem baffling, at least to me. Why, for example, would anyone wish to wear one which states "*Nothing Special*"? One which amuses me, however, worn by an attractive female, reads "*Mermaid off duty*".

Further along the road, the yet to be opened rapid transit light railway crosses over a heavily landscaped and attractive roundabout, and a new station housed in a large concrete shed seems to be nearing completion. Unfortunately, I will have to wait until my next visit to Macau before taking a ride on the sky train.

Tin Hao Maipo Temple, Macau

Taipa Bridge, Macau

Even where there is little traffic or few pedestrians, there is piped music at street level. This additional form of noise seems to be oozing out of manicured grassy verges of the gambling emporiums. It is getting too hot for me and I head back to the air conditioned Cotai Central. But just as I muse about the relative peace and quiet here, all this is shattered by a loud Disney style procession featuring a number of Bob the Builders and variations on Mickey and Minnie Mouse, plus several characters on stilts and a troupe of dancers, all of whom are parading noisily through the shopping mall. The children, of whom there are many, are thoroughly enjoying the spectacle – good harmless fun which seems to extend the aura of unreality which seems to permeate Macau.

Later on, at around a quarter to three in the afternoon, Sylvia and I go down to the mall for a snack. We are served by a delightful lady from Thailand; very slim but with a wide smile. She is keen to know our names and where we are from. She says she can make more money in Macau than back in Thailand, but she's a little evasive about whether she actually enjoys living here.

In the mall we book our ferry tickets to Hong Kong for tomorrow from two young ladies, Eunice and Sharon, who both say they are from Mainland China – *"from somewhere in the middle"*, they say. In addition to the tickets, they give us a map of the Hong Kong metro – the MTR – a Hong Kong street map and a bird's eye plan of Hung Hom station in Hong Kong, plus an envelope to put it all in. They even write the name of the station in Chinese characters to give to the taxi driver, but warn me: *"Hung Hom station is very complicated!"*

Just before four in the afternoon, a text message pings on Sylvia's phone; Carmen and Mario, the parents of two of our students who stayed with us a few years ago (Sénio and Claudia) will be outside our hotel lobby in ten minutes' time. We go into overdrive and just about make it down the lift in time to meet them, after a gap of a few years. Mario just manages to squeeze Sylvia's wheelchair in to the boot of his car and we set off to see some of the highlights of Macau.

"We are going to show you the greenest part of Macau", Carmen says – and after around 20 minutes we end up in what must be a special place, as it is the same square in Coloane where Nathan and Melodie took us on Saturday evening! Mario volunteers to

push Sylvia in her wheelchair along the same river frontage, and then we go for a coffee at the exact same place that we ended up in last night! I was half expecting the same waiter to come up and recognise me, but that doesn't happen. As well as drinks, Carmen orders 'nata' cakes which have a high proportion of custard and which I have to admit are delicious. (But they are not going to cure my diabetes.) She then orders two boxes full of them for us to consume on our long train journey to Beijing on Monday.

Tin Hao Maipo temple, perched on a hill, is our next port of call. This time, just Mario and I get out of the car and clamber up a pronounced slope to the temple entrance, where we encounter several stone dragons and a lot of red lights. Mario tells me that this temple was built to protect the local fishermen. But there are hardly any fishermen left in Macau these days, at least operating on a commercial basis. I wonder whether there is a temple to protect the gambling industry which has easily replaced fishing several times over as Macau's dominant industry.

The temple could be situated on the highest point on the island. It overlooks a beach and the open sea, with several islands in the distance, which are possibly part of the Hong Kong archipelago. There's a pleasant breeze up here, in welcome contrast to the heat of much of the day elsewhere on the island. From up here you can look in the opposite direction across the river into China as far as a forested ridge where several wind turbines dominate the skyline

Mario then drives us down the hill, past signs indicating the start of nature trails before taking a new road through a tunnel to the opposite side of the river, to land which is technically within China but where the Chinese authorities have allowed development to meet the needs of Macau as part of an area now administered by Macau. And so in this corner of Mainland China we drive on the left. We see the new Macau University campus, and I alight from the car, walk over to the side of the river and take photographs of the delightfully traditional Coloane riverfront on the opposite bank..

Vasco da Gama Square, Macau

Central Macau

We then re-cross the Pearl River before driving over the Taipa Bridge and enter the mainland part of Macau, or Macau-side as it is popularly known. Our restaurant, the Fado, is located in the heart of the ex-colony, overlooking Vasco Da Gama square, which is formally laid out with colourful flowerbeds, making an impressive sight as we look down from several floors up in the restaurant.

The Grande Lisboa casino, looking like a gigantic, golden dagger striking the earth, reinforced by its 'loud' lighting effects, contrasts starkly with the narrow streets and traditional tenement blocks which contribute to the colonial character around Vasco Da Gama square. I heard somewhere that the Grande Lisboa was constructed in defiance of the time-honoured principles of 'feng shui', and seeing the way it clashes with everything around it, it's not difficult to see why.

At the dinner table we meet up with two additional friends, Aurora (whom I always refer to as Senio's favourite aunt) and her friend Isobel, both of whom visited us when Claudia was living with us in our home. They talk a little about changes in the Macau workplace since the end of Portuguese rule in 1999. A good working knowledge of Mandarin is now a prerequisite for career advancement for all government jobs in the former colony, even though in Macau, as in much of South China, everyone speaks Cantonese as their first language.

A Portuguese chef from Braga comes over and explains how to cook a Portuguese speciality, *Bacalhao Bras*. Everyone wants to photograph him preparing this traditional fish dish. He tells me that he has lived and worked in Macau for the last two years; after another year he will probably look for pastures new.

It's been a great evening, even though we are pretty tired. Carmen and Mario have given us a great day in Macau and I think the icing on the cake has been the drive over the Taipa Bridge. There are bright lights everywhere as we are driven back to our hotel, making the harbour waters turn to red, crimson and purple. There is a real party feel to the ex-colony on this Sunday night. Back at our hotel, we spot the mini-replica Eiffel Tower radiating a luminous pink. *"Chaque un a son gout"* (each to his own taste) as one famous Frenchman once put it.

We manage to pack for the next leg of our journey by midnight and enjoy a relatively early night.

Contented diners, Hong Kong - Josh, Lai, Liz, Sylvia and Mike.

Contented diners in Macau: Isobel, Aurora, Mike, Sylvia Carmen and Mario

Monday 7 May

The Train to Beijing

Sylvia impresses me by getting up first, which gives me absolutely no excuse to lie in bed any longer. We are down for breakfast in the Yum Cha restaurant just before eight o' clock. The breakfast area is almost deserted and we are served quickly.

We are in the lobby awaiting Nathan and Melodie by 09:15, and we take in our last view of the entrance to the gambling tables; lots of bright lights, promising quick wins and instant happiness to go with it, together with guards and "no photography" signs just on the outside of the happiness zone.

Sylvia is expecting Nathan to arrive in the lobby any minute now. I decide to give him a call.

"*We're leaving home in about ten minutes*", he says.

"*He's so laid back*", sighs Sylvia.

A friendly receptionist with the delightful name of Lisa Li, looks out for Nathan and even offers to book a taxi for us to the Cotai ferry terminal. She tells us she lives in Guangzhou, about two hours away from here by car. She commutes every day (4 hours round trip), but prefers to live at home rather than rent anything in Macau. We have met quite a few Chinese nationals working in Macau, but it's clear that the property prices here are high compared to neighbouring parts of China.

Nathan eventually arrives about 09:50, but then announces that he has left his Chinese money (RMB) at home! But he's still very relaxed, saying that we have plenty of time. The taxi obligingly stops by at Nathan's flat in a traditional, quieter part of Taipa, where the three to four storey apartments are considered to be low-rise development. Despite work sheds and light industry across the road, his neighbourhood is still quite green in appearance. Ripe for redevelopment, I think, but this would be a shame. Nathan says land prices are escalating in Macau.

The Cotai ferry terminal is a new looking building, opened about two years ago. It is spacious and it's easy to find where you are looking for. Our high speed boat, a Cotai Water Jet, departs on time. The four of us share a table on board. It seems like most passengers fall asleep very quickly into the voyage.

As we approach Hong Kong, the amount of shipping predictably increases. After several outlying islands, the Hong Kong Island waterfront appears to our right, probably the most impressive waterfront in the world, dominated by the Bank of China Tower. The world famous, iconic Lloyds Bank building is now dwarfed by most of its neighbours, but it still surpasses them in its elegance. I hope that the Hong Kong planners continue to preserve its setting, including direct views from the Kowloon side of the water.

Our ferry comes to a rest at the China Ferry Terminal in Kowloon. A friendly guy helps us get into the right lift. He looks at me and says: *"You are the most handsome guy in the world!"* I reply: *"But the women never say it!"*

We take a taxi across Kowloon to Hung Hom Station, Hong Kong's main line railway terminus, where we will catch our train to Beijing. At one point in our taxi ride, the heavy traffic is held up by heavy goods vehicles manoeuvring into the main road in connection with activities on a construction site – to the sound of dozens of horns from impatient drivers.

Macau Ferry Terminal, Hong Kong

Our train for Beijing in Hung Hom Station, Hong Kong

Hung Hom Station sits on several levels, but it is spacious and easy to navigate. The railway tracks occupy the lowest of the five levels. We have time to order and eat some lunch before heading down to passport control and security. There is still an hour to go before our train is due to depart at 15:15 hours. In terms of entry into China, Sylvia must have been smiling more sweetly than me, because she gets a visa which extends until 3 November 2018, whereas mine runs out on 28 October!

As we move forward in the queue through the barrier for the train, Nathan enquires about the seat numbers on our tickets. The official shouts back: "*No! No! This queue is for the train to Guangzhou! Go Back!*" And the officials have to open the barrier again for us to re-enter the waiting area. A close shave!

Our train – Express Z98 – is hauled by a single electric locomotive at the head of around 20 odd coaches. I am slightly surprised that no one seems to mind me photographing the train, given the security conscious nature of the country. We have sleeper accommodation for this long trip, with just two bunks in our compartment, plus a chair and a washroom. Nathan and Melodie are nearby in the same carriage. Most of the sleeper coaches behind us have two and in some cases three bunks facing a further two or three bunks in the same compartment, so the first class accommodation we have booked counts for something.

We ease out of Hung Hom Station exactly on time and the train trundles slowly through the administrative area of Hong Kong for about 45 minutes. I miss the exact point where the traffic crosses over from driving on the left to the right (despite looking out for it), and before long we see the new 'rival' city of Shenzhen with its imposing towers. But it doesn't have Hong Kong's natural setting, even if its population, as one of China's new 'super-million' cities, now exceeds that of Hong Kong.

Sylvia and Nathan engage in a game of bubble-pop on Sylvia's i-pad. Nathan then asks a train steward why his bottles of beer can't go in carriage number 5, where he has noticed a fridge.

"*No*" says the steward.

"*Why can't you take some of the soft drinks out and replace with beers?*"

"*No!*"

"*Why not?*"

"*Because fridge not work*"!!

It's logical really when you think about it...

The train picks up speed after Shenzhen and we travel through a succession of industrial cities with occasional 'inliers' of traditional buildings, such as a few huts by the edge of a pond or some old tenement blocks. Some of the stations appear to be very new, revealing evidence of a lot of Chinese investment in its railways. We cross several sluggish rivers. Every now and then, factory chimneys appear on the horizon, along with the occasional temple or pagoda. Around five o'clock, the landscape becomes greener with several banana trees growing near the tracks.

There is a cloudy sunset as the train approaches the mega industrial city of Guangzhou (formerly known as Canton) with a population of over ten million souls. The train comes to an unscheduled halt in Guangzhou Station, and torrential rain starts to pour down on the roof of our carriage. We stay here for three hours, with no reason given, at least not in English, and with no one joining or leaving our train.

A train draws into the station on the next track and stops. The bunks on the neighbouring train are arranged on three levels, with occupants looking like caged birds. There is thunder and lightning, but still no explanation from the train crew for this hiatus in our journey. Then we hear a couple of loud jolts to our train and wonder whether they have added any coaches at the back. The next door train is also stationary for over an hour, as is another train which has arrived on the opposite side of us. It's all very mysterious.

During the second hour of our protracted stay in Guangzhou, we walk through to the dining car. We overcome the language barrier by pointing to pictures of food on the menu. The food isn't bad, and the 'picture' approach has been successful. It's still raining as we hear public information announcements, but they are all in Mandarin and none of the train staff can speak English. So we are none the wiser.

At 7:50, not far off three hours since the train stopped in Guangzhou, we pull out of the station on a section of elevated track. We pass thousands of apartment windows, mostly with their lights on and almost none of them with closed curtains; thousands of instant cameos on life in the city.

The rain continues as we pass through the suburbs, the factories, the tenement blocks, the markets and the warehouses of this mega city and it takes a long time until the train is passing through dark countryside.

Sylvia occupies the lower bunk and I decide to make do with the armchair and a blanket. We settle down to sleep as the train rattles on through the night.

Tuesday 8 May

The Journey Continues

I wake up in my chair in our compartment on board the train at around five thirty, to the sight of early morning mist and views of rice fields set in undulating countryside with scattered woodland. There are a few small hills and then terraced rice fields, which is pleasing to the eye (well, at least mine). We pass through some towns and cities, but they seem smaller than the urban conglomerations we went through yesterday and the overall feel is of a more rural landscape than hitherto.

We observe a lot of freight being transported by rail in China. Our train passes a couple of freight trains hauled by huge blue electric locomotives, waiting in sidings for their turn to gain access onto the 'permanent way'. Several fields have patches of brightly coloured flowers, with the colours looking artificial; I wonder whether these indicate burial areas. Farm workers walk or cycle between fields and we are passing through a tranquil part of China.

Just as we are being lulled into a sense of a rural idyll, we pass through a new town in the making, which I think is going by the name of Wu Chang Nan. Dozens of pencil thin tower blocks are under construction. The train stops in the town's new, palatial station, with no expense on its design and finishing seemingly spared. Several uniformed officials stand to attention along the platform, observing the train. No one gets on or off our train.

In the late morning we cross the vast, blue Yangtze River at Wuhan, another mega city. There is a long suspension bridge over the river to our left. We pass the city's pleasant municipal gardens, which are being attended to by an army of uniformed gardeners.

An hour to the north of Wuhan, the scenery changes back to open countryside. The hills are getting steeper. Water buffaloes plod through the rice fields and they seem to be giving free lifts to white birds, which resemble herons to my untrained eye. Our train then plunges through a series of tunnels, just as the scenery starts to become more interesting.

Around the middle of the day, I catch up on some sleep for a couple of hours. I wake up to views of largely flat countryside, but I can see a prominent rocky escarpment a couple of miles away to my left. There is a lot of sand and gravel extraction, with further evidence of sunken fields, where the land has been restored to agriculture, presumably following the gaining of the material, to fuel China's building boom. There is a slight heat haze.

At two in the afternoon we wander along to the restaurant car. Nathan has a special translator app on his phone and his first attempt at using it comes out with *"fried broccoli with fresh worries"*! Never mind.

We pass through more industrial areas. The occasional derelict factory is reminiscent of some of Hogarth's nineteenth century paintings of the British Industrial Revolution. These forlorn industrial structures by the side of the track indicate that there have been some casualties from China's extraordinary economic progress over the last few decades; it's not been plain sailing everywhere.

We see several new railways under construction, some on elevated concrete viaducts, maybe about 5-6 metres above the ground. There are signs of new development everywhere. This is a country on the move. Our train also passes several gated sidings, some with locomotives waiting to be let out on to the 'permanent way'.

Crossing the Yangtze River at Wuhan

Forbidden City, Beijing

Presumably there are reasons for these railway gates. Security seems to be a big thing in China.

As well as all the new development, we see new forests being planted. Travelling further north, the rice fields seem to be larger. Farm workers are walking through the crops, many wearing wide, yellow hats.

The train passes several more areas where fields are being excavated for sand and gravel extraction, which appears to have resulted in quite a large lake, together with artificial terracing of fields which have been restored to agriculture. Hopefully, the areas under permanent water will eventually become wildlife reserves, as has been the case in parts of England, in some cases very successfully. There are more signs of tree planting, which is always welcome. The landscape is now flat and stretches as far as the eye can see.

Several texts on my mobile phone are now flying back and forth between Zhiping, our friend in Beijing, and also with her husband, Lu Yang. The messages are about who is going to meet us and how late the train is expected to arrive at its destination. It looks like we are running around three hours late, directly attributable to our unscheduled stop last night in the rain at Guangzhou, which seems a long time ago now. The last of these texts says that both of them will be able to meet us, and the planned rendezvous is South Square, immediately next door to the station.

A word about Zhiping; I first met her when I responded to our doorbell and opened our front door at home on a Saturday morning in the early summer around twenty years ago. I was facing a young Chinese lady, who at that moment was a complete stranger to me. She said that she was not happy with her host family (actually it was a single taxi driver who was never at home) and asked if she could come and stay with us while she studied at a local language school. (She had heard about us from one of her fellow students, an Austrian lady who was staying with us.) An hour or so later, I drove round and helped collect her stuff from the taxi driver's home, and she moved in with us and became part of our family that summer. Little did we realise that, all these years later, she would be showing us around Beijing!

The skyline of greater Beijing now appears behind the last of the green fields. Our 20 plus coach train slows down and finally draws into Beijing West Station at 18:30, about 2,500 kilometres to the north-east of Hong Kong. The locomotive hauling our train has come to a halt a long way past a pedestrian barrier which I am not permitted to cross, so there's no chance of a final photograph or a chance to say hello and thank you to the loco driver(s).

Zhiping, our ex-student who has lived at our home on at least four occasions, and her husband Lu Yang, whom we are meeting for the first time, are waiting for us at the station entrance. They kindly take us all to our hotel, which involves hiring a taxi as well as the use of Zhiping's car. The four of us, plus Sylvia's wheelchair and several cases, comprise quite an entourage.

The roads in downtown Beijing at around seven in the evening are busy but not what I would call congested. The air also feels quite clear. Apparently we are about one kilometre from the city centre. Zhiping explains that cars can't be driven for seven continuous days a week in the city, in a bid to combat air pollution by having fewer cars on the road. She says she gets over the problem by owning two cars!

In the car, Zhiping tells us that she has just returned from a five-day series of business meetings in Shandong, about three hours away from Beijing by train, where she has been working on a lighting project.

Nathan and Melodie take another vehicle – a taxi, as everything and everyone won't fit into Zhiping's car, which is hardly surprising. Nathan says that the driver spent half the time shouting and sounding his horn at other inconsiderate drivers, and the other half of the time doing the same things himself!

Just after we all arrive at our hotel, Zhiping says she will return in 45 minutes' time, at eight o'clock and walk us to a nearby restaurant that she can recommend. Shortly after eight she returns and we all walk for about ten minutes along quiet residential streets in what seems to be an upmarket area of the city. Maybe the police station and the hospital which we pass contribute towards the quietness of the neighbourhood. The restaurant Zhiping takes us to specialises in traditional Beijing cuisine, including liberal helpings of dumplings. The meal is a great success; everyone enjoys their food.

It's a pleasant walk back to our hotel, the Holiday Inn, in Downtown Beijing, at around 9:30 pm. It's quite cool and dry and the streets are leafy and there is a pleasant taste of affluence. Although no one comments on the amount of food we have just consumed, Zhiping promises us a bigger dinner tomorrow evening! Zhiping's husband, Lu Yang, has had to stay at home to supervise their daughter's preparation for an important test the following day at school. Zhiping also says that Lu Yang's work is in the process of change, as the Chinese president Shi is combining the Communist Party and government departments; Lu Yang has his work cut out, apparently.

Nathan and Melodie plan to visit fabric shops in the city sometime in the next few days, but for tomorrow the plan is for all of us to visit the Forbidden City, which sounds a little scary, like we shouldn't be going there. We manage to get to bed just before midnight.

Zhiping and Sylvia, Forbidden City

Wednesday 9 May

The Forbidden City

I wheel Sylvia down from our bedroom to have breakfast. The chief steward comes over to our table and asks Sylvia what she would like, and then brings it to our table. Meanwhile, I have to forage around the dining area and get my own breakfast!

Sylvia, parasol and wheelchair, Forbidden City

Shortly after our appointed time, Zhiping arrives at our hotel to drive us to the Forbidden City, which is situated right in the heart of Beijing. The area surrounding the Forbidden City has a strict height limitation on development, which is entirely appropriate. Zhiping is calm and confident as she drives through the busy Beijing traffic; at the first police checkpoint, she gets out of the car, says something to the guards and the barrier opens to let us through. She does this for a total of three barriers altogether, so we end up driving inside the Forbidden City complex in a restricted parking area, away from the crowds. What power and influence the lady has!

Once we have parked, we have a rendezvous with our guide, who is a friend of Zhiping's called Micol. Sylvia is looking quite a picture in her wheelchair, sporting a wide-brimmed pink hat underneath a cream umbrella, and Nathan seems to have taken over the main responsibility of pushing his mum's wheelchair. Zhiping takes a photograph of Sylvia with her mobile phone and sends it to her husband, Lu Yang at work. He replies almost instantly, saying that he can see that Sylvia is a warm-hearted person. That just about fits the bill.

Before we explore the Forbidden City, it is necessary for me to find the public toilets (hoping they are not forbidden), due to a combination of my water tablets kicking in, a weak bladder and decrepitude. Inside the toilets, there is a simple picture/diagram at the entrance to each of the cubicles, accompanied by the words "*squatting position*", as the toilets are basically holes in the ground. But you need to have the strength and suppleness of an Olympic athlete to guarantee a satisfactory visit with a good outcome. And as for the toilet paper, where is it?

We enter the Forbidden City complex through the Merichan Gate, which has a design which includes the wings of a wild goose. In previous eras, the complex housed the imperial ruling family through two dynasties, the Ming and the Qing, who occupied the area exclusively from the fifteenth to the start of the twentieth centuries. During this time, only the imperial family and its entourage were allowed access to this place; hence to everyone else it really was a forbidden city.

Schoolgirls, Forbidden City

But today the Forbidden City is anything but exclusive and we are quickly mixing with vast crowds and feeling very inclusive. Across an expansive courtyard, we make for a traditional structure which is called the Hall of Supreme Harmony, which I am told dates from 1420 at the start of the Ming Dynasty. This building had at least four names; each time it was burnt down, which occurred during periods when there was civil war in China, it was rebuilt on the same spot and given a new name – Hall of Golden Bells, Hall of Venerating Heaven, Hall of Imperial Supremacy, and finally Hall of Supreme Harmony. There is a lot of talk about harmony on the information plaques, as we jostle through the crowds, unharmoniously at times. By midday it is getting hot, although there is a welcome slight breeze.

We walk through the Imperial Garden, and then, next to the Palace of Earthly Tranquillity, we come across a small, modest building, which we discover was the English teacher's residence. The obvious route to the next section of the complex has a 'no entrance' sign, strictly guarded by a man wearing a T shirt with the inappropriate caption of *"Break the rules"*!

The Northern Gate apparently accommodated the emperor's harem, and a plaque says that the girls who were accommodated here came from *"certain social groups"*, without spelling out exactly which groups fitted into this category.

Most of the imperial treasures were taken from the Forbidden City to Taiwan just after the Second World War and this may be the reason for a certain emptiness in some of the key buildings. I will be surprised if the treasures are returned to Beijing any time soon. My favourite T-shirt caption of the day so far has to be *"I don't need you – I've got wi-fi"*!

We cross a small river which protected the Forbidden City until the fall of the Last Emperor in 1911. A short distance away, at the foot of a wooded hill, is the Xing Zhan Gardens, named after a seventeenth century emperor who committed suicide in this place; a tree with a plaque indicates the exact spot where this happened.

I climb to the summit, where there is a small pagoda commanding an extensive view across the city; Zhiping accompanies me up the last two flights of steps. We discuss the Opium Wars in the middle and late nineteenth century and the British gunboat diplomacy at the time, undoubtedly helped by the fact that the Qing Dynasty was weak and in its final death throes. I reflect on the pretty awful British legacy of forcing the Chinese to trade in opium, partly, if my memory of A level history serves me right, to help Britain pay for its burgeoning demand for tea from India. Fortunately, all this happened over a century ago and as Zhiping says: "*We are friends now*".

As we descend the hill, she says to me: "*People are thinking that I am married to a much older person!*" I reply "*And they know I can't possibly be your father*". (Except through adoption I guess.) Zhiping says that the Last Emperor surrendered to an army of farmers who threatened to destroy the Forbidden City if he didn't surrender. So you could say he did it for China. His last refuge was the pagoda we have just visited. Nathan says this is the location where much of the *Last Emperor* was filmed.

Zhiping in Imperial Gardens, Forbidden City

Imperial gardens, Forbidden City

We catch a taxi back to our hotel, where we grab one and a half hours of rest before Zhiping picks us up for our evening meal. As we enter the restaurant, Zhiping's daughter Yjia comes up and gives us both a hug. She's a bit taller than when we first set eyes on her on Newton Abbot Station in August 2016. We are ushered into a small dining area, where Zhiping almost immediately decides the room lacks atmosphere. She then takes me to another, larger room and says: "*You choose*", although I suspect the choice has already been made! I suggest a location by the window, and eventually eight adults and two children (Yjia and her best friend Elsa) are seated round a sizeable alcove window table.

The circular glass centrepiece of the dining table can revolve through 360 degrees, enabling everyone to help themselves to all the dishes. I recall a story about a nineteenth century Indian Raj who had a circular table with a train going round, delivering food to the diners. Nathan says they have similar sushi trains in some Japanese restaurants. I really must visit Japan.

Quite a lot of beer is served and Lu Yang enjoys suggesting toasts, including one to "*Next year in Torquay!*" and then to "*Drinking *together in Torquay!"* I get the impression he may be coming over to see us next year...... Lu Yang also has a habit of refilling my beer glass when I'm not looking.

At one point, Lu Yang addresses me and says: *"You look like Sean Connery!"* Sylvia says: *"Where?"* Nathan joins in by saying: *"Like Sean Connery looks now"*, and gets a current picture on his mobile phone of the balding, white-whiskered actor. Only Zhiping comes to my rescue, saying that I look much younger than the present day Sean Connery. At this point, Zhiping is my only friend in the universe.

Lu Yang also tells me that a few minutes ago his friend John, who is sitting on the opposite side of our dining table, was in the middle of complimenting me on how well I was using chopsticks, at which point I dropped some food. So, farewell to the brownie points... John and his wife are the parents of Yjia's friend, Elsa, and they get chatting to Nathan's girlfriend, Melodie. John owns a fabric shop, and offers to let Mel visit his shop, as she is doing a fabric design course back home in the Philippines. It looks like Nathan and Melodie may spend Saturday looking at fabric shops, although Zhiping says that most of the fabric markets have moved out of Beijing to places like Hong Kong and Guangzhou.

Back at the hotel, as we enjoy drinks in the atmospheric coffee lounge, the conversation gets round to the Ming and Qing dynasties, which for some unaccountable reason develops into discussing the imperial harems. I blame Nathan of course for this. Nathan then has some difficulty explaining to Melodie who the eunuchs were, and she struggles to understand Nathan's definition, which he gives to Melodie as: *"men who have lost everything"*. On broadly the same subject, Nathan says he has just read a sign in one of the hotel toilets; instead of reminding people to look after their valuables, the sign says: *" Please look after your personal values"*, which is quite profound when you think about it. And on this philosophical thought, it's time for bed.

Thursday 10 May

The Great Wall of China

Zhiping collects us from our hotel at around 10:15 in the morning. The roads are still busy and we witness a couple of near misses at a major intersection; bikes and scooters are weaving in and out of each other's paths, and some cars are almost knocking down pedestrians. One old lady in a wheelchair is being pushed diagonally across – or is it through – the vehicular traffic at this complex intersection, and all of the traffic somehow manages to manoeuvre around her, putting her in varying degrees of potentially mortal danger and near misses.

The Great Wall of China at Shuiguan

But she emerges safely on the other side. Zhiping continues to negotiate the traffic calmly; nothing seems to phase her, serenity personified.

We travel northwards out of Beijing for about an hour and a half. We leave the urban area and drive into a mountain range. Then, there it is in the middle distance, coming out of the mist – the Great Wall of China (or at least part of it), snaking up the side of a mountain and down into the next valley and on again, bearing no relationship to the steep contours. This is indeed a 'wow' moment.

Although I have seen lots of pictures of the Wall in books and calendars, actually seeing the Great Wall 'in the flesh' for the first time is a surreal moment. The Great Wall stretches from the coast about 40 miles north of Beijing for over 1,500 miles to the north and west (i.e. a wee bit longer than Hadrian's Wall in the UK). On the way there, Zhiping tells us that her husband told her that he didn't need her in England next year – he has Mike! I'm not sure how to reply to that.

On the final stretch of road to the point where we will be visiting the Great Wall, a couple of cars sound their horns and overtake us, the second just missing a bus coming towards us. I think we are grateful to be alive by the time we reach our destination.

The place where we are going to get access to the Great Wall is a fort by the name of Shuiguan, which translates into English as 'Watergate'. I can see the gate but maybe the water has been culverted. We pass someone wearing an interesting caption on their T-shirt –*"Please punch me in the face – I want to feel alive!"* Zhiping succeeds in obtaining reduced prices for Sylvia and me. I am at the ticket kiosk, however, in the middle of my transaction with the ticket official, when a guy comes out of nowhere, shouting and throwing money at the woman whom I am in conversation with. To her credit, she ignores the guy, despite his continued ranting. Nathan comments that queue jumping by Mainland Chinese is a big problem in Hong Kong and Macau; it's a real clash of cultures.

Nathan, Zhiping and Melodie on the Great Wall

Nathan on the Great Wall

Situated near to the entrance of the Wall there is a small, landscaped garden with a statue of the Buddha at the far end. Work is being carried out to create a water feature to further enhance this pleasant open space.

We have told Sylvia that it is probably not going to be possible for her to actually get onto the Wall itself and that maybe she will have to make do with seeing the Wall from close quarters. But Sylvia has other ideas, and at the visitor entrance, she gets out of her wheelchair and single-handedly scales the 30-odd stone steps that lead up to the main concourse by the parapets of the Wall. The guards offer to take the wheelchair up the steps, but Nathan volunteers to do this. At the top, there is a straight, flat section of the Wall, and Sylvia is reunited with her wheelchair at a position slightly removed from a group of pushy saleswomen at their market stall. She says she is happy to stay here for a while whilst we go exploring.

At this point, Nathan eggs me on to join himself and Melodie to complete walking along the next section of the Wall, which leads uphill to another fort on the skyline, maybe half a mile distant. It seems a good idea at the time and I foolishly accept the challenge, which is probably not the most sensible thing to do at my time of life. Sylvia, on the other hand, is quite sensible and calmly sits in her wheelchair, observing us. Nathan and Melodie scramble up the steps like mountain goats, with me trying to keep up with them. The Great Wall connects a series of smaller and larger gates and forts, and the section of Wall where we are situated is wide enough for four people to walk easily side by side.

Maybe the word 'easily' is inappropriate to use at this juncture, because most of the section we "attack" comprises steeply inclining steps. Fortunately for me, a more recent addition has been the installation of handrails, including one rail (circa late twentieth century) running along the centre of the Wall. They may not look authentic Ming Dynasty, and they may not entirely harmonise with the rest of the traditional looking character of the structure, but they are a godsend to me!

The wall twists and turns, ever going uphill, and I reckon there are at least 500 steps for us to negotiate. These steps are separated by long vertical drops in places, and I find myself hauling up my body with the aid of the non-Ming Dynasty handrail. These steps must have contributed to gruelling route marches for the Emperor's soldiers when the protection of the empire from alien invasion was at stake. (And we know from the guidebooks that the wall was overrun by hostile forces on at least two occasions.)

The Great Wall

View from the Great Wall

The train is winning

When we reach our destination, Nathan tries to climb up onto the roof of the fort, sneaking past a guard to do so. The guard, however, is asleep, so that part of Nathan's plan isn't difficult; the guard is dead to the world, surrounded by dozens of plastic water bottles. But the gate up onto the roof is locked and Nathan's little scheme is thwarted. From our peak position before we start to descend, we can see the Wall ascending the hill on the other side of the valley, beyond the gate where Sylvia is still watching out for us. There are a lot more people walking up the Wall in the section beyond Sylvia's place of repose than in our direction. In fact, there are so many more people walking that far stretch, that I smugly deduce that our section must be considerably more of a challenge. I wonder if sections of the Wall are graded for severity, like you do for rock climbing. Ours must be graded very severe, me thinks.

Descending the 500 odd steps is a whole new challenge; again, I largely use the handrail, which is not just a help but a necessity. I think Sylvia has the last laugh here, waving to me from the luxury of her wheelchair on the ramparts below. But the icing on the cake is seeing a sleek, white inter-city train fighting the uphill gradient as we look down from the Wall to our left, where the railway ascends the valley in a series of curves.

We collect Sylvia from the lower ramparts. She walks back down the 30 steps or so, to the applause of the officials at the gate, who congratulate her on her great achievement of making it onto the Wall. And for Sylvia, with her Parkinson's condition and need of a right knee replacement in the coming months, it is indeed a great achievement.

Meanwhile, Zhiping has thought of everything. She has even brought sausages, bread and drinks, which we consume in a secluded patch of woodland, away from the crowds; a perfect moment for us to savour.

Shuiguan Fort

Yijia at home – this has to be painful

After lunch, Zhiping drives us back in the general direction of Beijing. I am in the front passenger seat, when I spot a train starting to overtake us to our left. I take a risk by taking a photograph, which turns out to be one of my more successful attempts – amazingly with no handshake in the moving car, I catch the white bullet nose of the train in my viewfinder, with a profile of Zhiping, driving between me and the train; a shot in a million!

Further down the road, we come across another gate in the Great Wall at a place called Badaling, where there is an impressively restored Ming Dynasty fort. We take a lot more photographs but give any more climbing on the Wall a miss. (Even Nathan and

Melodie decide on no more wall-walking, so the walk we did earlier this afternoon must have taken its toll on them as well as on me.)

We take some group pictures, and in a couple of them, a Chinese stranger poses with us, which for some reason really amuses Nathan. Sylvia and I, egged on by Zhiping, Nathan and Melodie (and maybe also by the Chinese stranger), buy T shirts which pronounce to the world that we have climbed the Great Wall. Whether I ever find the nerve to ever wear mine is quite another matter.

The Beijing rush hour slows down our early evening return to our hotel. It takes two hours to do the return trip. We find ourselves stuck in heavy traffic with the sounding of a lot of horns. For the first time I can actually smell the pollution which the city is renowned for. There's time for a short rest in the hotel.

At 6:30 pm, on the dot, Zhiping's husband, Lu Yang, collects us at our hotel and drives us the short distance (literally a couple of blocks) to their home, where we have been invited round for a meal. Zhiping and Lu Yang live in a compound of several apartment blocks, approached via an entrance barrier, which is policed by what appears to be private guards. Inside the barrier, it feels like a peaceful oasis in the heart of the city.

At our meal, which is an amazing combination of about a dozen dishes, we are introduced to Lu Yang's nephew, Gilbert, who recently spent nearly three years studying at one of the Edinburgh universities and who now works in Beijing. The only meal he recalls he enjoyed during his Scottish student days was fish and chips. His views on the Scottish climate are no more positive! But he does say that he enjoyed living and studying in that beautiful city.

Zhiping and Lu Yang's daughter, Yjia, entertains us by performing a dance routine, which includes doing the splits, which makes me feel pain just looking at her doing this unnatural act. She says she does the dance routine at school. Then she plays the piano.

Afterwards, Sylvia is persuaded to play the piano, at which point she becomes the focus of several cameras; it looks like she is surrounded by the paparazzi. Zhiping says Yjia plays table tennis; I must remember this for when she comes over and stays with us next summer (and maybe I need to practise as well).

At the end of our sojourn at Zhiping and Lu Yang's home, Nathan and Melodie decide to walk back to the hotel, but Zhiping kindly agrees to drive Sylvia and I back. We end the evening with a quick drink in the hotel's atmospheric bar, after which it really is time to sleep.

Chiang Kai Shek's Field Headquarters, Beijing

Zone 798, Beijing

Friday 11 May

Hutongs, the NCPA and an Arresting Development

Today, Nathan and Melodie are off exploring fabric markets in the city. Zhiping offers to take Sylvia and I to the main arts and performance centre in Beijing, with the prospect of a little shopping in the afternoon. She walks over to our hotel mid-morning and we take a taxi into the city centre.

Even at eleven o'clock in the morning, there is a lot of traffic in downtown Beijing. But we have a calm taxi driver who even whistles as he negotiates progress through the slow moving vehicles. Just to the south of Tiananmen Square, we are dropped off on the edge of an extensive network of narrow streets, called 'hutongs'. There are very few cars in this neighbourhood but lots of small, electric carts. Some of the streets are tree-lined and there are several flower beds. These old alleyways date back to the Qing Dynasty, and I think it's the nearest thing you can get to the atmosphere of Old Peking. There are several plaques commemorating historical characters; one such character, for example, is remembered as an important leader of the Board of Punishment in the mid-nineteenth century.

At one point a bridal couple pose for me to photograph them – and then I notice someone in the bridal party photographing me! The hunter is hunted. This is a very relaxing, laid back area with a satisfying absence of vehicular traffic. Zhiping says the area used to be the preserve of the leaders and rich people, the aristocracy, but all this changed with the Revolution. Everyone is free to come into this historic labyrinth these days, but during Mao's Cultural Revolution a lot of damage was wrought in this area, possibly due to its associations with the 'wrong' people in the class struggle. But Zhiping says the damaged buildings and artifacts are now being restored.

I step off one of the alleyways, through a door and into a secluded garden, where a plaque says this is an example of 'Peking style' character, dedicated to a famous Chinese author by the name of Mao Dun who lived in the early part of the twentieth century. The garden is certainly peaceful, despite its location in the centre of Beijing.

Then I spot a sign pointing to Chiang Kai Shek's field headquarters when he was in command of the Nationalists in China in the 1940s, before the Communists under Mao ze Tung drove him out of the Chinese mainland. In a way, I am surprised the complex hasn't been demolished and I think it's to the current regime's credit that it still stands and is remembered. But it's difficult to see into his former field headquarters; there is a closed gate with a few chinks of light showing what appear to be a parade ground and some traditional looking buildings behind. There is a view held by some Chinese that perhaps it's just as well that Chiang Kai Shek took most of the Chinese Imperial Treasure with him to Taiwan, where he set up his rival Chinese government, because they may well have been destroyed in the Cultural Revolution if they had remained in Beijing.

We break off to buy an ice cream from a small parlour. The sign in Chinese, so I am told, says: "*My mother says if you buy ice cream here, I can marry you*" - quite a promise resting on consuming something sweet! We continue strolling through the hutongs. We pass lots of high-end fashion shops, some with dancing girls enticing you to enter, with your heart but also your wallet.

After a couple of hours of exploring this wonderful, other-worldly area, we take a taxi to the Chinese National Centre for the Performing Arts. Zhiping is very keen to show us this place, and she even mentioned it in e-mails when we were discussing coming out here. The place clearly means a lot to her. On the way there, the taxi driver asks Zhiping if Sylvia and I are a honeymoon couple, as we look so very romantic! I'm not sure what to say, really.

The National Centre for the Performing Arts - the NCPA – is one of Beijing's masterpieces. Its huge curved roof is set off by a body of water, and it continues to delight the eye once we are inside the massive structure. The building is eleven years old and it looks even newer. And you don't have to be an experienced opera lover or an architect to be bowled over by its amazing architecture and atmosphere.

Much of the NCPA is designed like a museum, although there is also an auditorium. On one of the walls there is a saying by Xi Jin Ping, China's president, where he requires us to: *"remember the tradition, absorb the exotic and face the future"*. Zhiping tells us that Xi's wife, an accomplished opera singer, was more famous than her husband before he rose to the key political post in China. Apparently Xi is a keen opera goer and quite often attends performances here.

We are introduced to a young lady by the name of Trista, who works here and who is to be our guide for the next two hours. Her main task is to tune the pianos in the NCPA – all 68 of them, every day! She even says she enjoys her work, which has to be a labour of love.

In one hall, there is an exhibition of famous composers whose works have been staged here, and the list is inter-continental, even in such a relatively short time. This place has certainly put Beijing on the operatic world map. I learn for example that Rossetti wrote 75 operas, and there's a lot of background stuff on the composers' life histories, on the political context of their lives, who they were friends with, their romances, interests and a lot else besides; plenty to interest a non-musician like me.

The hutongs in Old Peking   Zhiping and Yijia, mother and daughter

Trista suggests that we have a break over complimentary coffee and cake in a spacious and airy cafeteria. In the middle of the afternoon, this place is almost deserted. From where we are relaxing over our drinks, we can see a huge wooden object in the shape of a boat, big enough for several people to sit on it. But no, it is a Chinese stringed instrument, with a distinct resemblance to a boat. We also pass by beautiful models of opera houses from the Qing Dynasty, with exquisite detailing. No attention to detail is spared.

Inside the Chinese National Centre for the Performing Arts

Pyramids – Aida stage set

Perhaps the *piece de resistance* in the entire NCPA is the stage set for Verdi's Aida, which was performed here recently. There is a huge wooden boat, complete with a gigantic figure of a ram's head at the bow of the vessel. But it gets even better as you step inside; as you walk into the ship's interior, you step into the ancient world of Egypt. Here you can see models of the Pyramids at Giza, but superimposed upon the pyramids are moving images of a man, followed by a line of around twenty camels; antiquity meets the digital age. We are lost in our imagination, inside a stage set, inside an amazing building.

Maybe the highlight in this place for Sylvia is being able to see an orchestra rehearsing on the main stage, but the toughened glass through which we are viewing the scene makes it impossible to hear what they are playing. It still looks impressive.

It is clear that no expense has been spared in the construction of the NCPA, which comes complete with marble floors, its huge, arched roof, fabulous acoustics, lots of exhibition areas for operas, concerts and fine art work, not forgetting the attractive water features outside. The building looks fantastic from the outside and its interior does not disappoint. Judged by the number of internationally recognised performers who have given concerts here since 2007, this place has really put China on the world stage for the performing arts.

We are so taken with the NCPA that we stay here until its doors close to the public at 5pm. Then we drag ourselves away from this amazing place and take a taxi to Tiananmen Square, the nerve centre of Beijing and by extension, China. It is necessary for us to go through a security check, and for the second time today we have to show our passports.

Tiananmen Square is vast by any standards, and the buildings which define its edge, including the Great Hall of the People and the National Museum, seem far away from where we are standing across a sea of space. The many people walking and standing in the square look like ants, dominated by its sheer scale. It is easily more spacious than Moscow's Red Square, which is dominated more by its iconic buildings. But its vastness is impressive, and it probably comes to life when there are military parades and national celebrations.

At 5:30 in the late afternoon, the square is crowded, but I notice only a handful of European tourists. Just as I am beginning to be mesmerised by the ethereal atmosphere, we are brought up sharp as we witness an arrest, just a few metres in front of us. Three uniformed men are dragging a woman, at speed, into a police van. I quickly decide not to take any photographs, and it's just as well because the arresting officers pick on an onlooker, take possession of his camera and delete the photographs he's just taken of the incident, and maybe more. The whole episode is over in a matter of minutes.

Great Hall of the People, Tiananmen Square, Beijing

Vastness of Tiananmen Square

Zhiping says that the woman was trying to make a complaint against the President, rather than being a common criminal arrested for, say, pickpocketing. The whole thing is quite a shock to the system, for me at least. And passing quickly on, as it were, Zhiping stops a passer-by and asks him to take a photograph of the three of us. The man even moves his own children out of the way so they do not interfere with the picture, and he seems quite professional in the way he takes the shots; Zhiping has chosen well. His family is amused when I then ask if I can take a photograph of them, although they pose dutifully for me.

A short distance further on, Zhiping gets chatting to someone else in the street (and people say I am a chatterbox...). It is a Tibetan couple, who again turn out to be very friendly. But here on the street, they are reluctant to talk about the political situation in Tibet. While we are waiting for our pre-arranged taxi, two other cab drivers draw up and offer us a lift. Zhiping says this is the black market and the black market prices are much higher than the official taxis.

We are back in our hotel by six. I get on the phone to Nathan, who says they are in a café opposite the Workers' Stadium where there is a football match tonight. He and Melodie have one more market to visit and plan to return to the hotel by nine. Sylvia reflects that this afternoon was supposed to have been reserved for shopping. Maybe this will happen tomorrow afternoon?

We take our evening meal in the restaurant on level two of our hotel. The staff are all friendly, but none of them speaks English. Words like water and dessert have them flummoxed. We are the only diners in the restaurant for most of the time we are here, alone in the midst of 20 dining tables, and I am not really surprised. The food is fine, but overpriced.

Nine o'clock comes and goes without sight or sound of Nathan and Melodie. They turn up around ten and are clearly exhausted. We catch up briefly over drinks in the hotel bar before it's time for bed.

Saturday 12 May

The Summer Palace, Ice Cube and Bird's Nest

Zhiping collects us from our hotel at around eleven in the morning. She drives us to the Summer Palace, where the ruling emperors stayed whenever the weather got too hot in the centre of Peking. Upon arrival at the palace gardens we are introduced to some of Zhiping's friends - a lady called Lilly and her daughter, Jessie, who is a friend of Zhiping's daughter, Yjia, and Jessie's elder brother by several years, called Eddie. We are then joined by Zhiping's husband, Lu Yang and daughter Yjia, so we have grown into a sizeable group of eight, although this is not unusually large in comparison with some groupings in the vast crowds that have made it to the Summer Palace this morning. Nathan and Melodie are off doing some exploring on their own today, although we are all meeting up for a pre-arranged evening meal.

Lu Yang is sporting a Germany football shirt and he is also keen to push Sylvia around in her wheelchair; I never tire of offers like that. The Summer Palace is situated some way out from the centre of Beijing in what appears to be a largely rural, pleasantly undulating area. The palace complex sits on an artificial but natural looking hill, known as 'long life mountain' at the edge of Lake Kunming, quite a long way from the entrance to the gardens, making a long walk/push necessary for us to get to the palace area. The lake looks full of ferries and pleasure boats and, as it is a public holiday, there are people everywhere. This is certainly a popular destination for Beijing residents and you can see why.

Half way along the banks of the lake, we catch a ferry to the palace buildings, which cuts out a lot of walking. The boat passes by an impressive 150 metres long stone bridge, known as the 17 Arch Bridge, for a reason not difficult to fathom. It was constructed in 1750 in Emperor Qianlong's reign. Five hundred very life-like stone lions guard the bridge. There is also a stone ship at the water's edge, just before the quay where we disembark, but what purpose this feature had, I'm not sure.

Once on 'long life mountain', it looks a long way (in terms of wheelchair pushing) up to the main Summer Palace residence of the former emperors. Instead, we follow a course along the water's edge and then we step/push into a long, semi-open corridor or veranda, which is over one kilometre long. All along the upper parts of the walls of this corridor, as far up as the ceiling, there is a continuous series of pictures, maybe a hundred, maybe more.

Eddie assumes the role of our personal guide, and he is good at it. I am informed by him that many of the pictures in this corridor are scenes which stem from stories told by Confucius, and they are all based on Chinese folk lore. Many are quite striking, and I am fortunate to have Eddie alongside to explain them to me. This is like walking through the soul of China, and I can't think of any equivalent historic/artistic/cultural feature in the UK. It is an amazing experience, and I am probably taking too long appreciating it, as each picture is special and many of them are haunting in their beauty and/or the story they are telling. Most of the others in our party are way ahead of us by now. I take a lot of photographs of these beautiful paintings.

We walk out of the corridor and into a garden area. This is known as the Garden of Clear Ripples, which as the information plaques announce, was destroyed by Anglo-French forces (under the command of Lord Elgin, the one who famously nicked the Greek marbles). The combined army burnt down almost everything in the Summer Palace in 1860, presumably in connection with the earlier Opium Wars, about a century after it was beautifully created. Fortunately, most of it has now been restored, and being descendants of these Franco-British invaders doesn't seem to place us in any danger from angry crowds a century and a half later.

Summer Palace Gardens, Beijing

Seventeen Arch Bridge, Summer Palace

We walk through a complex of former imperial buildings, noting that the Hall of Benevolence and Longevity initially didn't have much longevity, because the British in 1860 didn't show much benevolence and burnt it down in the Opium Wars. But it has been lovingly restored.

Scene from the Long Corridor, Summer Palace

Scene from the Long Corridor, Summer Palace

One of the key people who bankrolled the rebuilding of the Summer Palace in the late nineteenth century was the Empress Dowager Cixi, an amazing character who rose from being a concubine to the effective ruler of China for nearly five decades. (If that's not an achievement, I don't know what is.) If she ever issued cheques, she would have had difficulty writing her entire name (The Current Divine Mother Empress Dowager Ci-Xi Duan-Yon Kang-Yi Zhao-Yu Zhuang – Cheng Shou-Gong Qin-Xian Chong-Xi of the Great Qing Empire) on a relatively small piece of paper. She divides opinion to this day – was she a cruel despot or an effective ruler? Was she Margaret Thatcher and Imelda Marcos rolled into one? The etchings show her finger nails stretching at least twice the length of her fingers, climaxing with narrow, sharp points. You had to be careful shaking hands with her no doubt, or it was a trip to the local A&E.

Stone ship, Summer Palace

We pass by some dragon and lion statues; Zhiping says they were erected to provide for protection against evil spirits, although she says this as though their role continues to this day.

Eddie does much of the wheelchair pushing and we talk a lot as we wheel our way through the Imperial complex. His spoken English and knowledge of the UK and the British political scene is unparalleled among the people I have spoken to on our holiday; in fact in my experience, his spoken English is second to none. I would go so far as to say that his spoken English equals that of any other Chinese person I have ever spoken to, and he is only in middle school. (Later in the day, when Nathan asks him where he acquired his near-perfect English accent, he says he modelled it on the BBC costume drama *Downton Abbey!*)

Protective Dragon, Summer Palace

As well as explaining a lot of the pictures we saw in the long corridor about half an hour ago, Eddie tries to educate me in the succession of Chinese dynasties. From what he tells me, it seems that there was a 'Golden Age' between the eighth and tenth centuries AD when art, literature and good living flourished. The concept of a united China, however, emerged some time earlier, around the fourth century AD. But the unity was punctuated by periods of division and in-fighting in addition to attacks from outside China.

Later in the afternoon, the number of visitors to the Summer Palace seems to have increased even more, and we notice several tour groups, each following their leader who is holding up a brightly coloured flag on a stick. On two occasions, I hear roll calls being taken, to cut out stragglers. The sheer numbers of people make progress pushing Sylvia's wheelchair quite challenging, especially when faced by a phalanx of people following a tour group leader, spreading out across the entire walkway. On occasions, we hold our ground and the tour groups split up around us like the parting of the Red Sea. In the melee, a lady asks Zhiping if she can have her photograph taken with me. The people who make kind comments about my appearance tend to be either women of a certain age or men!

Zhiping announces, towards the end of our visit to the Summer Palace, that we have walked nearly 10,000 steps; which is less than the 16,000 we totalled yesterday. But today is more tiring, due I think to the sheer numbers of people milling around in the grounds of the Summer Palace. It must have been a whole lot quieter when the emperors held sway. Another possible reason is the pollution; it has been noticeable all day, and it must have an effect. Amongst other things, it has made my photography more difficult because of the haze. Nevertheless, it has been a great experience for us, despite the crowds and the pollution, and I leave the Summer Palace having learnt so much about one of the world's great civilisations as well as it having been such an enjoyable experience.

Back at the hotel, we have an hour and a half before we are due to be collected for our meal out with Zhiping's family that Sylvia and I are officially hosting or bankrolling, or whatever the expression is. Nathan and Melodie have bought a posy of flowers which they give to Zhiping when she arrives at the hotel. It's a nice touch and one that Zhiping clearly appreciates, and definitely worth a photograph by me.

When we arrive at the appointed restaurant, we discover there are ten of us for the meal – Zhiping's family and Eddie and his mother Lilly and sister Jessie who were with us earlier in the day – plus Nathan and Melodie, Sylvia and I. But it makes for a lively and lovely evening. Zhiping says she is putting me at the head of the table, but as it's a circular table, it is debateable whether it actually has a head. I am sandwiched between Sylvia and Lu Yang.

Bird's Nest, Beijing Olympic Site

Ice Cube, Beijing Olympic Site

At the end of a great meal, I thank everyone for making our time in Beijing so enjoyable. Nathan comments that it has been the best Chinese food he has ever tasted; praise indeed.

But the evening isn't finished yet. After a few goodbyes outside the restaurant, at around nine o'clock, Zhiping takes Sylvia and I plus Nathan and Melodie to see two iconic buildings - the Ice Cube and the Bird's Nest – which were the focal points of the Beijing Olympics. We walk through fairly relaxed security controls and there are a lot of people strolling around the Olympics site on a pleasant warm evening. Both the Ice Cube and Bird's Nest are illuminated, together with the structure that housed the Olympic torch. A nearby office building also joins in the illuminations jamboree, with ever changing colours shooting up and down a series of vertical paths on the side of the structure. The atmosphere of the site is still electric, all these years later, clearly testament to a great Olympic Games here in 2008.

Nathan informs us that in Macau they have constructed a casino that is virtually a replica of the Ice Cube, but they deny any similarity, saying that the colours are different! As Nathan says, it is a tad disrespectful to copy an Olympics iconic building for what is in essence a gambling den.

Zhiping then drives us past Tiananmen Square where at ten o'clock there is still a lot of traffic driving on the eight lane highway running past the square.

Sketch of the Hutons, Beijing

Sunday 13 May

Zone 798

It's a hot day with clear skies; and there's not much pollution hanging over Beijing at the moment. Nathan left early this morning to go to South Korea to renew his visa (he's returning here this evening), but Melodie is coming with us. In the car, Zhiping talks about her work. She says she reports to her main boss once a month. One of her responsibilities is to make sure her four workers are paid; I'm quite glad I don't have that responsibility.

We are off to visit Zone 798. In the run up to the 2008 Olympics, the China Government, in order to cut down the pollution, decided that a lot of industry should be closed down in Beijing. One complex of former factories was taken over by an artists' colony, and the place now exhibits a cacophony of styles architectural, music and retail outlets. There are lots of overhead pipes (for heat and power) which have been preserved from the time when Zone 798 was a thriving network of factories; the pipes add an extra dimension to the ambience as does the stylish and colourful graffiti. Of particular interest to Melodie are the chic fashion shops and boutiques. One fabric shop is blasting out 'teenage boogie' music, à la Little Richard.

In the pedestrianised central square we discover a street café and order a variety of drinks from the French-American owner. There is what I can only describe as mood music in the background, but it feels appropriate for the surroundings. A slight sensation of spray from a water jet coming from a nearby flower box is welcome in the heat. Zhiping observes that the atmosphere in this area is more like Europe than China.

| Zone 798, Beijing | Zone 798 |

Some of the arts and crafts businesses started life as joint venture schemes with companies from outside China – mainly European – and Zhiping says she only learnt of this place through a German commercial contact. Around the central square there are impressively colourful murals. In an art exhibition just off the square, I read a definition or exposé of good design – which is: "*innovative; makes a product useful; aesthetic; helps a product to be understood; unobtrusive; honest; durable; thorough to the last detail; concerned about the environment; and there should be as little design as possible*". As a working definition it seems to say it all. My lofty design-centred thoughts are brought down to earth by a passing T shirt which states: "*Merde, il pleut*"! Fortunately there is no real rain at the moment, and definitely no need to swear.

One of the former manufacturing sheds has been preserved from its previous life. The room is vast with its concrete arches and high roof, and it lies mainly empty, save for a few surviving examples of the original machinery and industrial equipment which is preserved in steel cages. There is a Chinese slogan on one of the walls, which I am informed translates as: "*Long live Chairman Mau*".

Zhiping drives us back to her home in the middle of the day, where Yijia is doing her homework. She has 60 maths questions on one page of her school book, and she has to complete all the exercises in five minutes. No pressure then. Is this kind of training the secret as to why Chinese people, in my experience, are always so good at maths, almost without exception?

China Railway Museum – former railway station

Zhiping, slightly reluctantly I think, agrees to take us to the national Railway Museum, just off Tiananmen Square. The museum is housed in a former main line railway station which was opened in 1876 and which then closed its doors to rail passengers in 1959, presumably because it was no longer large enough to accommodate the demands of the growing railway industry in China, such as the requirement for longer trains and more of them. It bears the hallmarks of classic nineteenth century French railway architecture and it reminds me of the Musée D'Orsay in Paris (another former rail terminus converted to exhibition space – in that case into an art gallery, which has similar dates, closed for similar reasons and has a similar looking façade, and houses arguably the world's greatest collection of impressionist paintings).

On the ground floor we see an introductory information board which sets the background for the development of railways and their growth in China. The information starts with the phrase: "*Although railways were invented in another country......*" I tell Zhiping that I have a good mind to delete the words 'another country' and insert the words 'United Kingdom'!

China's Rocket in the Railway Museum

However, the museum information does state that in 1865, a couple of British businessmen visited the Imperial Chinese court and exhibited a life-size railway locomotive, which initially caused panic and riots among the people. There is a model of the Chinese 'Rocket', looking quite similar to George Stephenson's locomotive of the same name, but dated 1876, some forty plus years later.

Within a few years, however, of the visit of the British businessmen, the museum informs us that railways took off in China, to the point that the country now has the most extensive rail network in the world with the highest number of stations (over 50,000) and the most freight and passengers carried. The museum also announces that in 2016, a weekly freight service from Shanghai to London was introduced, something I have been following in the British press.

Lu Yang and Zhiping, our unofficial Beijing tour guides

The museum houses some interesting models, including a CRH3 'Hexie' electric multiple unit, popularly known as a bullet train, which can reach speeds of 350 km per hour, and the HXD3B high-powered electric locomotive at the head of a coal train. We will see plenty of these powerful looking blue locomotives on our travels next week.

Qianmen Daje pedestrian thoroughfare in Beijing

There are photographs of impressive bridges and there is a huge picture, taken in snowy wintry conditions, of the expansive marshalling yards at Suifen He – the tracks stretch into the distance – at the Chinese border with Russia. At this point, Zhiping comes alive and tells me she is involved in a street lighting project in that place. She tells me that she did not know this museum existed, but says she has enjoyed it and will definitely be visiting it again. Another railway convert...

We leave this interesting place and wander into a broad, pedestrianised (with the exception of a slow moving tram) thoroughfare – Qianmen Daje - with a lot of shops and restaurants. We are assailed by a variety of cooking aromas and enter the Qaanjude Restaurant and order a set meal for four people which includes Peking Duck. There is also Jasmin tea, for which I am acquiring a taste.

This is another superb meal at a popular restaurant; the minute we get up from our table, our seats are taken by another group, such is the level of its popularity. Outside the restaurant, in the cooler air of the pedestrian thoroughfare of Qianmen Daje, we look for post cards and pause to take in the movement, sounds and colour of a bustling part of downtown Beijing. Zhiping must be reading my thoughts, and she says: "*The difference between China and the West is that the West is clean, well ordered and boring; China is dirty, untidy and amazing!*"

I find somewhere that sells post cards just off Tiananmen Square, while we are waiting for a taxi that Zhiping has just ordered. But because of my deliberations, Sylvia and Melodie take the pre-booked taxi and poor Zhiping has to wait with me for another one.

We drive past a building with what sounds like Christian music emanating from it and a lot of people leaving what must be a church service. Our taxi driver doesn't take any prisoners with his driving – any driver attempting to veer into our lane gets the full headlight treatment and solid sounding of the horn for several seconds as he cuts past them at 50 mph. No one steps out of line. There is no way I'm going to fall asleep in this taxi.

Zhiping comes round to our hotel at 9:15 pm with some presents and we say our goodbyes; we couldn't have asked for a better host and guide to Beijing and we feel truly privileged, and it has also been great to meet and get to know Lu Yang and of course to see Yjia again. Nathan returns from his South Korean day trip at 9:30, complete with the necessary papers. We spend the rest of the evening packing, as we are going to be on the move early tomorrow to the city of Xian.

The Bullet Train to Xian

Our taxi driver to the station collects us from our hotel at the chillingly early time of 07:30. We drive through heavy traffic even at this hour, immediately behind a vehicle displaying a sticker which reads "*Turn off your fxxxing high beam!*", which is really in my face. Far more offensive than any high beam.

Our first guide of the day, Lulu, takes us through a maze of passages at Beijing West Station. She says, looking at me: "*The guide in Xian, Isaac, is handsome, but not as handsome as you!*" To which Nathan says: "*James Bond!*" To which Lulu replies: "*007!*" Thank you, Nathan.

Once we are seated by our bags, Nathan asks if he can go out for a smoke. Lulu says: "*Come with me – I give you Chinese cigarette!*" Upon their return, Lulu gives us an impromptu Mandarin lesson and her enthusiasm is infectious. We take some photographs of her – she is clearly very happy about this – and she asks Melodie to send them on to her. I tell her that she would make a great teacher of Chinese in the UK; she should believe in the dream.

Our train to Xian is a CRH3 bullet train, just like the one we saw in the railway museum yesterday (well, a little bit bigger). It is sleek and white and it has, as its name implies, a bullet shaped nose. We are in the lead coach of 16. The interior of our carriage, which is business class, is very plush and spacious, with reclining seats.

Drinks are served. I notice that Sylvia is looking very pleased – this is a world apart from our train to Beijing from Hong Kong.

We ease out of the station and the train rumbles past huge rail yards and a locomotive depot. There are extensive areas of cleared land with only a few older buildings remaining. No doubt the plan is to introduce higher storey development here. We cross on a bridge over a wide, sluggish river and then we are racing past rice fields. The pollution seems to be worse today, possibly as we are travelling on a working day, judging by the thick haze which limits distant views.

We settle into our seven-hour train journey. I start writing post cards. Sylvia is playing games on her i-pad. Melodie is sketching a dress design on her tablet. Nathan is playing games on his smart phone. No need for conversation right now.

Our first stop is at a place called Baodingdon, and as the train slows down, serried ranks of tower blocks come into view across the rice fields. It's another gleaming, white, concrete, modern station, although a lot of effort has been put into greening the place.

Another stop and another modern station, at Shijazhuang - I count 20 platforms beneath a huge steel and glass edifice. Nathan and Melodie hop out onto the platform for a smoke and I stretch my legs and take in the vastness of the station. Our train leaves after a 20 minute stop. Tracks fan out in all directions, some of them elevated and some under construction.

We traverse pleasant areas of farmland, punctuated by clusters of single storey structures, which could be accommodation for the farming community. Again, we see several sites of gravel extraction, fuelled by China's rapid development growth. One such site has led to a few pools and a lake.

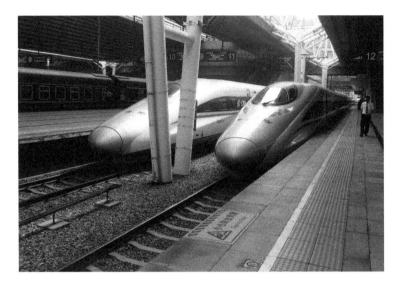

Bullet train to Xian at Beijing West Station

Scenery from the train en route to Xian

At Xingxaidong Station, the landscaping is extremely impressive and the town has a pleasant and green appearance. The open fields are still mainly growing rice, but there is some intensive market gardening. Our next stop, Hebidong, is another town with a lot of construction projects. It almost seems like there is a race on to see who can put up the fastest development with the tallest towers.

At the town of Zhengzhoadong, there is what can be described as a choreography of railways on viaducts, criss-crossing each other gracefully and joining up in yet another large, spacious, airy, modern station. On the station platform, Nathan says that the Chinese investment in their railways puts us in the UK to shame. It is certainly impressive. I learn sometime later that all these stations with 'dong' at the end of their names are indicating that they are on the east side of the towns they serve; that 'xi' means west, so Xian was the western capital of China; that 'bei' means north – Beijing is the capital in the north of China; and that 'nan' means south, and that Nanjing was the southern capital of China at one time. This stuff keeps a geographical anorak like me going for hours.

The landscape starts to change. It gets hillier and then we are in a mountainous region, an area of small rural settlements, forested areas and, alas for my interest in the lie of the land – tunnels. The train emerges from tunnels on a couple of occasions, crosses incised river valleys with spectacular views, but as I rush to take a photograph we plunge back into another tunnel; I am undone by Chinese efficiency.

We also pass a couple of huge factories with giant pipes, cooling towers and a lot of smoke and steam rising into the atmosphere. We are climbing the contours and the temperature is also on the rise. At the town of Luoyangloggmen, where the station only has a mere five platforms, the temperature has risen to 35°C. Then it's more heavy industry before the rice fields begin again. In the hillier terrain, the rice is grown on terraces, which to my eyes lends a special beauty to the landscape.

At Sanmenxianan I spot a few yellow maintenance locomotives, the same colour as they are in the UK, before we cross a few forested gorges. We see a newly built long, concrete bridge across a wide river with sandstone cliffs on the far side. Several fields have what look like religious shrines. The train pulls out of the next station, Huashanbei, into an area of steeply sloping mountains and traditional temples. There is also a limestone escarpment with some terracing on the lower levels; then it's past more power stations, industrial areas and yet more cities, which never seem far away from the countryside.

As our train pulls into the city of Xian in the early evening, our next guide, Isaac, recognises us from the picture Lulu sent him on her mobile phone from Beijing, and of course he knows which carriage we are in. He's a small guy with a big smile (and brain) and, as we are about to discover, he has a lot of knowledge and a passion for Chinese and world history. He informs us that we are the entire tour party; there was me, expecting a group that we were about to join! So we have the tour company, in the form of Isaac, all to ourselves!

It takes 50 minutes to drive from the station, through a city of 9.3 million inhabitants (which Isaac describes as a middle sized city, even though it is the size of London) to our hotel – the Grand Park, Xian. Nathan tells us that Zhiping told him that the driving in Xian is even worse that in Beijing, and after a few minutes in Isaac's car, we believe her. There are several near misses, one seemingly in the order of inches.

In the city centre we slow down and pass through an arch on the north side of the ancient and impressive medieval looking city wall. We continue through the compact historic core and then drive through the south wall, and into the hotel reception area, which is within eyeshot of the city's ancient fortifications. Isaac says Xian was the capital of China prior to the Ming Dynasty; in fact it was the capital for six dynasties.

Sylvia and dog, Xian

Our hotel is impressive, or at least the reception area is, with a fountain and a grand piano. But the plush carpets slow me down when I am pushing Sylvia in the wheelchair. Sylvia seems to like it, however. Nathan and Melodie have been out exploring and by seven o'clock they have discovered a restaurant in a nearby office block. The office block has a huge central hall, and on the ceiling there are action shots of crashing waves, which is impressive and maybe the only chance much of the population so far inland will ever get to see of the sea in action, as it were. We take the lift to the sixth floor, where there is a note warning us – "*no pressing button randoming*".

The sixth floor is devoted to restaurants. One of these eating establishments has a variety of sea creatures in large glass (or at least see-through) tanks, in line with the nautical theme of the main hall ceiling. All manner of creatures are waiting to be chosen and cooked, including huge sea frogs, turtles (which really cuts me up), lobsters, several species of fish and shellfish. Customers point to the meal they want and a few minutes later they are eating it freshly cooked. Something about this strikes me as chilling; is it the immediacy of death? Why am I more concerned about the fate of the turtle than the demise of the sea frog?

In another restaurant that we choose, on the same floor but somewhat distant from the aquarium, I happily eat fish as part of the dishes served to us. But the menu is only in Chinese, and we are bailed out of extreme embarrassment by some chatty Australians who recommend a local chicken speciality (as well as the fish).

We emerge, in pleasant, subdued heat, onto the main square in the city centre, which has been taken over by community dancing. Apparently the dancers, in folk dress, come from the province of Su Jian, which is located next to Mongolia. A local man approaches me, greets me and asks if I like China and Xian, and I answer truthfully in the affirmative. He says he lives and works here in Xian. At one point I think he is asking me about a present, and then I work out that he is wishing me a pleasant stay, which comes as a bit of a relief. Then he walks down the steps and joins in the dancing.

Further along the square, couples are doing something akin to European ballroom dancing, again to live music. Then, even further on, there is a band, verging on the size of an orchestra, accompanying a group of dancers with colourful flags. Their rhythm is infectious and we stay a long time watching the dancing and enjoying the music.

There is yet a fourth group of dancers accompanied by piped music and finally, at the edge of the square, opposite our hotel, a lone guy sings folk songs in Mandarin to haunting, minor chords; it is a beautiful sound, even though I can't understand a word he is singing.

The singing, dancing and general celebration and merriment in the town centre puts us in a happy mood. Xian has a soul after all.

The Terracotta Army

Xian – the city of Western Peace - rose to fame, apparently, in 221 BC, when Emperor Chin of the Han Dynasty amalgamated seven kingdoms, started building the Great Wall of China as a show of strength and introduced widespread irrigation. According to Isaac our guide, nobody liked him, but at least he got jobs done and he was quite a reformer.

We are now, at the start of the twenty-first century, in another great development period in China. Isaac says that because there is no private ownership of land, quick decisions on new roads and railways can be made, and as we have seen, China today is really galloping ahead in the world development stakes.

Street dancing, Xian

Today, Isaac is driving us to see the Terracotta Warriors, which have really made this place world famous. Before taking us to the excavations, we stop by at a factory retail outlet, which is doing a brisk trade in selling newly made terracotta warriors, some over six foot high. The larger warriors can be made in seven days and the clay is fired at 900°C. One of the staff at the outlet says: *"You can ship a general back to your own garden!"* This is not exactly what I came out to China for, and I resist the temptation of showing off a terracotta warrior in our back garden at home.

Sylvia does force my wallet open, warrior style, to pay for a miniature terracotta soldier, but I'm not even sure where we are going to put him back home! Nathan outdoes me and buys two – one for Melodie's mantelpiece in Cebu in the Philippines and one for his TV stand in Macau. Whilst in the retail outlet, I use the toilet; the Chinese may have invented paper but the connection between paper and toilets seems to have been lost somewhere down the line.

We drive from the retail outlet to the centre where the terracotta warriors were unearthed a few decades ago. We pass a huge statue by the side of the road, depicting a Tang emperor dancing with one of his concubines, seemingly without a care in the world. This suggests an age of happiness and a flourishing of art and cultural freedom. The Tang Dynasty is commonly acknowledged as a Golden Age in China, lasting from the seventh to the tenth centuries AD, when paper, printing and gunpowder were invented.

We also pass an artificial hill which accommodates Emperor Chin's (full name Qin Shi Huang) mausoleum. This was the king who united China from a number of separate kingdoms in the third century BC, started the building of the Great Wall of China (arguably the greatest construction project of all time) and unified the Chinese language (arguably an even more challenging project). He also commissioned the terracotta warriors to protect him in the after-world. He may have thought he needed some protecting because by all accounts he didn't treat his people well and he may have thought that the population would seek revenge after his death; who knows, as much of this is speculation, although I find it fascinating.

High ranking terracotta warrior   Serried ranks, but each warrior is unique

Our lunch as usual is on the over-plentiful side, but nevertheless difficult to turn down. The highlight of our lunch is the demonstration of the traditional Chinese tea ceremony, which we share with a chatty couple from North London (They explain that they went to a similar event in Sri Lanka, where the presenters were absolutely insistent that adding milk to tea was not only not a good idea, but an absolute 'no no'!). Our hostess lets us try several brands, including Ginseng Oolong tea, Lychee Black tea and Chrysanthemum tea. I am not a tea drinker, but the ginseng tea seems OK, even to my taste buds, and my ears prick up when the lady says that it is good for the immune system.

The story of the discovery of the terra cotta warriors is one of the great archaeological stories of all time. The warriors remained hidden under the ground from the third century BC until a farmer was digging in a field for water in 1974 – and the warriors were discovered by accident (and the farmer was able to stop farming almost immediately for some strange reason). The field was transformed into a major archaeological site and the museum complex now accommodates the areas where archaeologists are still digging; there's still a lot of work to do.

Tang Dynasty statue – emperor dancing with one of his harem

Ancient drawbridge, Xian

In the main reception area there is a map showing the location of the imperial palace, constructed between a hill and a river, which I am told is classic 'feng shui'. The map also shows where the warriors were buried – to the east of the palace where it was thought the enemy might attack. According to Isaac, the people who dug the cemetery were then buried with the warriors in order to keep the location secret, but if this is true, it does seem to be a tad ungrateful for all their work. Also, a sizeable amount of mercury has been found near the tombs, and the rumour is that a river of mercury ran round the warriors' resting place to keep people out. Well, the plan succeeded until 1974.

Another ominous find is a lot of charcoal and it does seem that someone tried to set fire to the warriors about the time of Emperor

Chin's death, which has been verified by the use of carbon 14 dating. But this is not really surprising as many people hated him and it would no doubt be likely that some would have wanted to settle scores as soon as he died.

The first pit was excavated in 1976. Some soldiers were found standing, but most of the timber clad tombs had decayed; soil had fallen through and crushed many of the statues, which were damaged or destroyed by the weight of the earth over time. The warriors are divided into generals, infantrymen, archers and horsemen, and were buried together with some of their horses. The horses are life-size; the warriors a little larger than life.

The archaeological site/museum is very crowded and I initially wonder how Sylvia is ever going to see anything. But I needn't have worried. Sylvia's wheelchair pusher, Mr Chew, makes it his mission to wheel Sylvia to the front of every display. He takes no prisoners as he cuts a wheelchair-shaped swathe through the crowds. Nathan calls him the 'snow plough' as people scatter like the parting of the Red Sea, which amuses us all greatly, especially Nathan.

We start off looking into Pit 2, which has only a few warriors left standing; some have been taken by archaeologists for display elsewhere, including an exhibition in Liverpool. Pit 3 accommodates the strategic command centre, which includes several horses for taking messages quickly. Most of the warriors in this pit have lost their heads, which Isaac thinks was by tomb robbers for money. But in Pit 1, there is a huge display of warriors – around 6,000 of them.

It's difficult to put into words the frisson of excitement and wonder you experience when you stand in this archaeological site, facing the ranks of these amazing, larger than life men of war, created to defend the emperor in the afterlife. Even though they were created in terracotta, they face you as a formidable force; you wouldn't want to argue with a single one of them in a dark alley, let alone with such a huge army. They are indeed amazing creatures with a fearsome dignity and severe beauty. I feel privileged to have caught a sight of them, in the flesh as it were, and been able to marvel at one of the archaeological wonders of the world.

We also witness what is referred to as the Phase 4 signing ceremony, with dignitaries being interviewed in front of TV cameras. Clearly there is a significant amount of work still to do before all the warriors' secrets are completely unearthed, and Phase 4 is clearly something to do with that.

The work of reassembling individual warriors continues, working in some cases with tiny fragments. They are in various states of repair. Some have been carefully covered with cellophane. There is still some excavation going on and there is a view among many of the people 'in the know' out here that there could well be further discoveries. Who knows how large the terracotta army really was? Maybe Phase 4 will provide some of the answers.

We agree to have a group photograph overlooking Pit 1. After people keep walking across the field of vision, Sylvia's wheelchair pusher, Mr Chew, takes matters into his own hands and he physically blocks any one from getting in the way of the picture.

On the one hand, the sheer mass of warriors, especially in Pit 1 is impressive. But at another level, the individual detailing of the faces and bodies of each warrior is also amazing; no two warriors are exactly alike – they are all individuals in their own right. In this sense they are very human. We are also privileged to have Isaac as our guide, as he knows so much; he answers all our questions, his English is good and his enthusiasm is infectious.

Around half past four in the afternoon, we walk back to the museum car park, and we are home shortly after six. Heavy traffic on the return journey gives us time to enjoy the mountain views; a large pagoda stands on one of the summits, and it is connected to the city via a cable car, which is maybe a trip for another time.

The four of us decide to go into the historic core of Xian for our last meal together, before Nathan and Melodie fly back to Macau via Hong Kong later tomorrow. We walk through the South Gate of the City Wall, but only after I literally run across four lanes of traffic to photograph the drawbridge of the South Gate Fort being raised over the moat. I then race back across the rapidly approaching cars, vans, motorbikes, scooters and cyclists. I return to the others safely but a little out of breath. Nathan, who is amused/impressed by all this, gives me a high five. But Sylvia turns to Nathan and says: *"Don't encourage him!"* I'm amazed that I can still run after being on my feet all day long.

Old Xian

Once inside the city walls we discover a tranquil street (as in terms of vehicles) with a few shops but no restaurants. But as we turn a corner we come across a succession of bars, several with live performers. We opt to enter a restaurant called Bavaria, and once inside, Nathan and Melodie successfully order German beer which is to their liking. Food wise, we order sausages, fish and chips, salad and noodles – a strange combination but it fits the bill right now. Nathan is impressed that I can recognise music by Ed

Sheeren and Coldplay whilst we are eating; there's life in his old dad yet. All in all, we are pleased with our sojourn at Bavaria. The two serving girls are friendly and the bill is reasonable. It has been a pleasant final meal together.

Old Xian

The café on the opposite side of the street has an unusual sign in English: "*Please be patient with the bar tender. Even a toilet can serve only one asshole at a time*". This doesn't appear to come with a Chinese translation; is this because the Chinese are better behaved and more patient in bars I wonder?

There are final hugs in the hotel as we will be leaving early in the morning (07:00) for Chengdu, and Nathan and Melodie fly back to Hong Kong later in the day. Our packing is completed by midnight, but work continues on a demolition site right below our bedroom window until the small hours.

Wednesday 16 May

Travelling to Chengdu

They are still working on the building site next to our hotel bedroom when the alarm sounds at the unearthly hour of 05:15. Sylvia struggles to get ready before her medication which she takes (first set of the day) at 08:00 hours. To my surprise, Nathan and Melodie are downstairs in the hotel lobby waiting for us; there was absolutely no need for them to get up early on our account, as their flight to Hong Kong is not until the afternoon. So, it's final hugs time, and the four of us become two for the purposes of this diary.

Isaac also arrives at the hotel early and he's on hand to help Sylvia into the people carrier. We give a final wave to Nathan and Melodie; hopefully we will see both of them before too long. Isaac discusses British and European history with us as we make our way to the station through the Xian rush hour. The guy is passionate about his subject and we have been privileged to have him as our guide in Xian.

As we approach the station, it gives me the impression of a modern version of a traditional Chinese hut, but it's the size of a small airport; a sensitive combination of the traditional and the contemporary. We say farewell to Isaac and step on board our bullet train, which seems to be even more spacious and comfortable than the one from Beijing.

Terracotta horses, Xian

Terracotta warriors in Command Centre

After about 20 minutes, the train leaves the flat lands behind and plunges into a series of tunnels through a mountainous area. Some of the rice fields we see from the train are terraced and there are people working knee deep in the water and mud. Whatever the stark reality is of working in rice cultivation, the scene from the train looks beautiful and harmonious.

At Guengyan station, there is another plethora of railway tracks on display and there are several diesel and electric locomotives, some coupled to long freight trains. Several lines, including ours, are shooting off into yet more tunnels in this mountainous area.

Some small valleys have been transformed into progressively smaller terraces; the ones located higher up the valley sides are looking like steps to heaven. Several of the tunnels we travel through spill us out onto bridges crossing attractive rocky valleys but before I can get my camera out, we are back into the darkness of yet another tunnel, which is quite frustrating. The railways are too efficient and direct for an antediluvian photographer like me.

The railway crosses over a river just downstream of a dam. We cross a forlorn trickle of water meandering through wide expanses of gravel which once formed the submerged river bed. It is like the lifeblood has been gouged out of a once-vibrant natural force.

We are served a rice meal on the train, aircraft style. But as normal, we are eating too much. I do find it difficult to resist food that is served up for me, whatever the situation; a pitiful lack of self-discipline.

Our train arrives at our destination in Chengdu, at another large, mini-airport styled station, mid-afternoon and five minutes early. As we alight onto the platform, a woman comes up to me and asks if I need help, to which I reply: "*No thanks*". But then the penny drops. I say: "*Are you Della?*" She is Della, our company rep whilst we are in Chengdu! She is quite chatty, and tells us she is a "*local girl*" and that she hasn't even travelled as far as Xian.

Once we are aboard the people carrier, Della tells us that Chengdu is famous for the hibiscus tree, which was promoted by the concubines of a famous emperor, who then planted the tree throughout the city.

Della asks us about our backgrounds. Sylvia tells her that she was a music teacher. At this point, Della breaks out into an impromptu Chinese folk song as we drive through the central area of Chengdu. I am then thinking that maybe she will help us find some authentic Chinese folk music on a CD, maybe in a market. So far I have been unsuccessful in coming across anything beyond contemporary popular music on this holiday.

We arrive at the Chengdu Hangfu Sunshine Hotel, which is pleasant and welcoming, and it has full disability access for Sylvia. We are on the twelfth floor. Looking out onto a busy traffic intersection, it certainly has the edge over the demolition site we overlooked from our hotel bedroom in Xian.

Della comes up to our room and we agree to meet tomorrow at 09:30 am in the hotel lobby. For some reason, I then say: *"Or we can meet in the bedroom?"*. Della replies: *"Oh, I am so sorry – of course we can meet in the bedroom"*. Me and my big mouth – I then say that this was just a throw away comment and a totally confused Della eventually agrees to meet us in the hotel lobby. As she leaves our hotel, she turns and says to me: *"You are a humorous guy; I like you!"*

After taking a rest, Sylvia and I go for a short walk/push through the city centre. As in much of China, the surfaces of the pavements have braille markings – great for the visually impaired but the disjointed levels are quite a challenge for the wheelchair pushers!

As we are progressing along the pavement, an old lady with few teeth and a big smile gets chatting to us, but unfortunately for us it is in Mandarin. Despite the language barrier, we detect warmth in what she is trying to convey to us, even if we can't understand a word of it. Della says the woman is almost certainly welcoming us to her city, which is such a sweet gesture. It gets me thinking whether anyone in the UK would go out of their way to welcome foreigners whom they encounter in the street.

The streets around the hotel where we go for our walk comprise mainly shopping frontages and the immediate area looks reasonably well off. Della had told us earlier in the afternoon that the city has not prospered to the same degree as Beijing, as it does not have the same political influence, but she accepts that things are getting better.

We meet up with Della again in the hotel at 7pm. She takes us to a place which she says she thinks we will enjoy, where they serve the local Sichuan cuisine. In the UK, this cuisine has a reputation for being very spicy, and Della asks the waitress to make our meals less hot than they would normally be, which is thoughtful of her. Over our enjoyable meal we get chatting about our families. Della is married to a professional photographer and they have a four year old daughter, who lives some of the time with her grandparents in the countryside.

Della says she studied English and Japanese at university. But she hasn't been to either England or Japan and she didn't have any Japanese people helping her with the language. Interestingly, she says she admires much about the Japanese attitude towards technology, an area where she feels China still has a lot to learn. She accepts that not all of her fellow citizens have the same attitude towards Japan after all that happened during the Second World War and in other conflicts, but she thinks it's time to move on. I think we could go on talking for several hours but Sylvia is starting to tire and at about nine o'clock we say goodbye and look forward to a good day's panda watching tomorrow.

Later in the evening, I wander down to the reception and ask for coffee and powdered milk sachets. I am told that getting a coffee is OK but not the milk. I reply by telling the people on reception that we had powdered milk sachets upon arrival at the hotel. Then they ask me: *"What is a sachet?"* I try to explain, but clearly I am not making a good job of it. One of the hotel staff gets out his pocket translator.

"*Ah!*" he says, with his eyes lighting up, "*You want sugar!*"

"*No, I want powdered milk sachets*".

"*Oh, you want tea?*"

At this point I have a brain wave. I tell them I will retrieve the used sachet from the bin in our hotel bedroom; I leave them, hurry up to our room, I rummage through the waste bin, I find the discarded dried milk sachet and then I take it down to them in the reception. At this point, the light dawns. Five minutes later, a woman knocks on our bedroom door and hands me four coffee and four powdered milk sachets. I really must learn a few more words in Mandarin, like for powdered milk sachets.

Serious shopping, Zone 798

Thursday 17 May

The Giant Pandas

We hear thunder in the early hours and it is raining as we set off from our hotel in the people carrier for the panda reserve. Our route takes us past the aftermath of a multiple car crash, the worst we have seen in China. Then we have to slow down to avoid the deepest section of a localised flood which covers our carriageway. I spot a T shirt being worn by someone at the side of the road, with the caption *"Sick and Tired"*, which somehow seems appropriate in the dismal weather and flooding. But just when I start to think we are in for a panda washout day, the rain stops and the temperature is cool and pleasant.

The Giant Panda Reserve enjoys a peaceful, rural setting, some distance away from the city of nearly 15 million souls. And it feels like a thousand miles away from bustling Chengdu.

At the entrance to the reserve, there is a huge board, on which is written in English (there is no Chinese translation):

All things bright and beautiful
All creatures great and small
All things wise and wonderful
....
By Cecil Francis Alexander

The fourth line, which is critical to the meter and the meaning of the traditional English hymn, is absent (*The Lord God made them all*), and the imbalance of the remaining three lines must strike at least some English speaking Chinese reading it as odd. But there it stands, greeting everyone entering this place.

Which one was I eating?

Walking into the spacious reserve, we find ourselves in a bamboo forest, which seems to have the ability to soak up the impact of lots of people and still give out the ambience of rain forest in rural China. Before we get to see any pandas, I am intrigued by seeing a huge peacock straddling the upper reaches of a tree, and it is also very well camouflaged. I can only remember seeing peacocks strutting around on gentrified lawns back in the UK, and certainly never up a tree!

We spot a family of four beautiful, black and white Giant Pandas, two adults and two young, in a clearing. They are separated from the humans by a low wall and a ditch; there is not an electric fence in sight. But there are signs in English as well as in

Just one bamboo shoot more

Chinese, warning people not to get too close to them, as their 'cuddles' could prove fatal. Sylvia remarks that they could easily cross over these insignificant obstacles if they so wished and I agree with her. But, thankfully, they show absolutely no interest in doing this. The adult pandas give a new meaning to the term 'laid back'. One of the young pandas scales down the side of a tree almost effortlessly, to the great amusement of the human onlookers. My camera is working overtime taking pictures of these wonderful creatures.

The adult pandas are lying on their backs most of the time, chewing one stick of bamboo after another. Apparently the nutritional value of bamboo is miniscule, which forces them to eat almost continually when they are not asleep. One of the adult pandas in particular gives a Paddington Bear expression as he/she nonchalantly chews through a bamboo stick, randomly spitting out the husky bark, and you can almost imagine a jar of marmalade in its paws.

We are transfixed, watching these cuddly and amiable looking furry blobs enjoying their continuous brunch. This is without doubt one of the highlights of our time in China. These animals are majestic and yet so relaxed in this peaceful environment and time seems to stand still as we just observe them doing what comes natural to them in a truly authentic setting.

Entrance to Panda Sanctuary, Chengdu   Beautiful Giant Pandas

Inevitably, there is a museum which tells the story of the reserve. A screen show is well attended. However, when the filming moves onto the subject of mating and a series of graphic images appear, leaving little to the imagination, there is an impromptu mass exodus of Chinese families, leaving behind a small remnant of viewers (Shades of No Sex Please, we are Chinese).

The reserve was founded in 1987 and now has the largest panda population in the world. We are also informed that some pandas have now been released from the reserve back into the wild in the remoter parts of China.

The reserve is an extensive forest environment with plenty of space for the pandas to live, move and have their being, which for a panda means continually eating, interrupted by sleeping. The bird life is also interesting; we spot a bird with brown and orange wings, grabbing leaves by the beakful. There is also a pond with bright red and yellow fish, possibly carp, judging by their size.

Unlike Sylvia's wheelchair pusher at Xian, the guy today is no snowplough. On occasions I decide to make a path for him and Sylvia to follow, otherwise Sylvia isn't going to see much of the panda action. And on occasions, the pusher clips a few heels, resulting in irate stares.

After a couple of hours we leave the reserve. It has been a totally relaxed experience with a lot of slow walking/pushing, and stopping for long periods, observing these delightful creatures.

Della locates a restaurant where we stop for an hour or so. Again, it's far too much food for a sensible lunch, but the variety of Sichuan food, including spiced chicken, is impossible to resist. Sylvia says the diet starts when we leave China. I'll back that. Once back in the city, the driver stops at a shopping mall, and Della and I search for a new backpack to replace Sylvia's, which is worn out and is no longer safe to carry valuables. After quite a long search we are successful and I purchase a smart dark green backpack which I have to admit I rather like.

Jin Lee Alley- traditional village in Chengdu

Chengdu city centre

In the afternoon, Della takes us to a traditional village within the city, called Jin Li Alley and which I am informed dates from 220 AD when China was divided into three kingdoms which were at war with each other. We enter the village off one of the main city streets, next to a beautiful park. We feel like stepping back in time, into a network of narrow streets full of small shops and kiosks, thronged with people and which is thankfully car-free; there are shades of Dagon Alley, right out of the Harry Potter books. The only problem we have is making progress with the wheelchair through the crowds and across the cobblestones. Many of the roofs are pagoda styled, covering stone or timber structures. There are red lanterns everywhere, and many multi-coloured flags and pennants; in all, a colourful and lively scene.

A couple of streams flow through the village, and these are crossed by humped-backed stone bridges and flanked by a few trees. We stop and recuperate in a small café in the centre of the village and drink passionfruit juice. Our driver, using the translation APP on his mobile phone, wants to know if we like his city. I tell him that I am certainly enjoying this part of the city.

On the way back to our hotel, at my request, the driver takes us through Temple Square, which defines the city centre for the 15 million or so people who live in this metropolis. In front of the city hall stands a gigantic statue, in white, of Chairman Mau, with his right arm raised aloft. Surrounding Chairman Mau there are pleasant, well laid out, landscaped gardens. The relatively quiet traffic conditions within the heart of the city seem like the eye in the storm in relation to the heavy traffic congestion in much of the rest of the urban area.

Later, we go for a final evening meal with Della, in the Xiaolong Kan restaurant in the city centre. Della recommends the local 'hotpot' as she calls it, but this one certainly doesn't originate from Lancashire. But it's good, even if the hot, spicy nature of the food makes me feel like a nuclear reactor. In the centre of the table there is a bowl of water surrounded by a larger bowl, full of spicy vegetables. The bowls are heated to boiling point from a source under the table. Our food is then cooked in these bowls – pork, vegetables and potatoes, all of which are delicious.

There isn't a European in sight, and Della says the restaurant staff are curious about who we are and where we come from. They are very chatty at the end of our meal, although meaningful conversation is limited and conducted entirely through Della as interpreter. The irony is that my Mandarin APP on my phone can't work in China because it is linked to Google.

Just after we leave the restaurant, I realise once I am out on the street that my glasses are missing. I must have left them on the dining table in the restaurant. I take the lift back to the restaurant, but I can't remember the correct floor for the restaurant and I initially walk out of the lift at the wrong level and into a dark and deserted car park, with absolutely no one in sight. But by the time I reach the right floor for the restaurant, I discover that the staff have already returned my glasses to Sylvia on the pavement below!

On the way back to the hotel we stop to watch a dozen or so lady dancers of a certain age, accompanied by hauntingly beautiful Chinese/Sichuan music. We drag ourselves away from the dancers, say farewell until the morning to Della, and then retire to finish off our packing and go to bed.

Time to relax

Rough and tumble

Friday 18 May

The Train to Shanghai

We make a good start; we are up before seven and down for breakfast shortly before eight. Della collects us at half past nine and the traffic on the way to the station is light, as we have mercifully missed the worst of the rush hour. Della sings to us in the people carrier; she tells us it is a farmer's song, which is apparently on the repertoire of China's first lady, who is a nationally acclaimed opera singer. She asks us which music we like and says that she is a big fan of Adele; I tell her that we heard someone singing an Adele song in a bar in Xian a couple of nights ago.

Chengdu North Station is huge and of course modern. We arrive with over an hour to spare, which is the normal required time on Chinese railways. The electronic, state of the art departures board shows 20 trains scheduled to depart in the next 90 minutes. Every one of these trains is indicated as being on time; trains currently boarding are highlighted in green and those where the carriage doors are closing in red. The system is running like clockwork, to use an English phrase; in fact, better than clockwork.

While we are waiting for our train, Della shows us photographs of her four year old daughter on her mobile phone. Then she manages to accompany us through security and shows us into our carriage; she says it is the first time she has been able to do this and actually board a train, and seems to be quite pleased with the experience. We are in coach 1 of the bullet train to Shanghai, situated next to the driver's cab. It's time to say goodbye to Della, who has been an excellent guide and a good singer.

Our express train to Shanghai glides away from the platform exactly on time at the scheduled time of 10:57 hrs. Just outside the station there is an amazing clover leaf junction, not of motorways but of railway tracks, similar to a motorway intersection in the UK, such as at Spaghetti Junction on the M6 motorway on the edge of Birmingham, with rail tracks crossing over each other at different levels and angles; another part of the Chinese railway miracle.

Train announcements are made in Chinese and English. One of these states: "*Smoking is strictly forbidden everywhere on the train- appropriate action against violators will be taken by the railway police, who will take action in accordance with the regulations*". This sounds a tad scary to me, and I'm not even a smoker. At every station we stop at on our journey, dozens of passengers, nearly all of them men, alight onto the platform for a quick smoke, presumably beyond the reach of any police action.

For the first couple of hours we follow our route back towards Xian, through the same tunnels, rice fields and heavy industry. I walk down the train to find the drinks counter, which is staffed by two young women. They tell me: "*No coffee!*". I pretend to cry, and my pathetic attempt at humour at least makes them laugh. Most of the train carriages are crowded, with three seats on one side of the aisle and two on the other side. Several seats are occupied by an adult and a child. As far as I can make out, we are the only non-Chinese on the train.

Again, I am mesmerised by the rice fields that we can see from the train. The landscape appears to be so delicately balanced. Some of the fields are like small swimming pools, with the water precariously close to cascading over onto the field on the next contour below. In other fields, groups of workers, many with conical hats, often stooping, are attending to the unglamorous business of rice cultivation, although the images from our 300 kph bullet train are highly romanticised.

Sylvia boarding the bullet train for Shanghai

Rice fields from the train

Our journey to Shanghai takes us back through Xian, passing several high-rise apartment blocks under construction on the edge of the city. We pass more elevated railways on concrete viaducts and other railways under construction. There are more huge railyards, and more construction and development, confirming that Xian is another big city on the move.

Someway to the east of Xian, we stop at a relatively small station. Our stewardess indicates that we have a ten minute wait, so I alight onto the platform with the smokers. I am surprised by the strong wind, perhaps heralding a change in the weather. Within minutes of our train starting off again, it is raining and the wet surfaces of the adjacent highways are glistening. We are cocooned from the weather by the train; we can observe the beauty of the rain's visual effects without being soaked. By chance or design, the coming of the rain coincides with a much greener landscape. We pass a windfarm where the blades of the turbines are racing around in the strengthening wind. From inside the train, it's looking quite autumnal out there.

Hillside tableau at Suzhou   The same tableau, a couple of minutes later

The train enters another urban canyon by the name of Zhengzhoo. There is also quite a lot of demolition of older, or substandard, office blocks – or maybe the sites are seen to have the potential for building significantly more storeys. We stop at another huge station at 5:25 pm, and a lot of people board the train. There is evidence of significant tree planting in this place, and the train passes an ornamental boating lake. Around seven in the evening, dusk starts as we progress eastwards in a huge country with a single time zone.

Just before it gets really dark, the train stops at an historic town called Suzhou. I notice something interesting and I alight onto the platform to get a better look and to take photographs of this phenomenon. Overlooking the station, on the side of a ridge, maybe up to a couple of miles away to my left (although it is difficult to estimate the distance with certainty) there is a procession of huge characters including two horses and carriages, which are illuminated on the darkening hillside.

What are they celebrating? Is it a political, religious, civic or social procession? The tableau is similar in some ways to the huge White Horse which is drawn or etched onto chalk down land in Wiltshire, back in the UK and which is clearly visible when travelling on the Great Western Railway. But the difference here is that the characters I can see from the station at Suzhou continually change their colours – green to blue, orange to red, completely absorbing my concentration. It looks to me like a procession straight out of the Ming Dynasty, but I really have no idea what these wonderful characters portray.

By 7:30, as we pull out of this station, the night is black. The train stops several more times before terminating in Shanghai. Just before this, I finish reading Paul Theroux's the *Great Railway Bazaar*, which is kind of appropriate, as this is the last of our long train journeys in China.

Our Shanghai guide, Grace, spots us through the carriage window and gives us a wave. Her porter wheels our six items of luggage at near Olympic speeds, followed by Grace pushing Sylvia in her wake, with me hot-footing it, bringing up the rear – through a very crowded station concourse, which is also colossal. Somehow we don't collide with anyone, and we leave the station around ten-thirty.

Our driver, Mr Lee, takes us to our hotel, which is situated in the centre of the city. The traffic is relatively light and we are in our hotel bedroom before midnight.

Saturday 19 May

Urban Planning and Jessica

We wake up to a wet morning in Shanghai. Mid-morning, Sylvia and I venture out of our hotel onto the city streets. We make it along Fuzhou Road, one of the city's main thoroughfares, in the direction of the Shanghai Urban Planning Exhibition Centre. (It's actually spelt 'Center', but as an Englishman I can't cope with this American spelling.) This turns out to be a glorious and inspirational celebration of town planning in a purpose-built structure on five levels, in a high profile location next to People's Square, which is about as central in the city as you can get. It is high on vision and visual impact if a little short on factual and quantifiable detail in places. But it makes for a great couple of hours, and there's even a pleasant café on the top floor, where we draw breath for half an hour.

Shanghai comes across as a colourful, dynamic and bustling city, ready to take on the world. And the Exhibition Centre certainly makes town planning an exciting career prospect for all the young people who are visiting this wonderful place, many of whom seem to be taking a keen interest in the exhibits on display. Sylvia is also really interested in much that the exhibition has to offer, so she tells me.

Some of the exhibits are futuristic, such as an 'Imax' type experience, where you stand on a small dais, looking at a huge screen, and you see scenes from the city, flying over them as it were. I really have to hold on to the rail to stop myself from losing my balance and falling over. Other exhibits celebrate the past, including an array of black line drawings by an artist by the name of Li Shoubai, of downtown Shanghai in the 1920s and 1930s. Each drawing highlights a single building or feature in red within a largely black and white context, such as a street scene, and we spend a long time standing and admiring them.

People's Park from the Urban Planning Centre, Shanghai

Model of Downtown Shanghai, Urban Planning Centre

Perhaps the most moving exhibit depicts the earthquake in Wenchuan in western China in 2008. Photographs show the extent and scale of the devastation; there's a picture of a highway sliced in half in a mountainous area, and another of a historic church with its bell tower partly collapsed. Perhaps the most harrowing of all is a scene of a school classroom, taken immediately after the earthquake, with school bags lying in the rubble and the contents of desks and drawers scattered all over the floor or what was left of it. But a new town at a place called Beichuan has started to heal the wounds, and there are shots of smiling children playing in the town square. Sylvia requests me to take a photograph of a picture of two dogs posing with their owner in the recently constructed new town.

One of the themes of the exhibition could be about making things happen in Shanghai. We peer down over a huge model of the city. From this vantage point we can see that, although the city is not afraid to develop clusters of very tall buildings (many by the river), there are extensive areas of relatively low-rise housing, maybe as low as two to three storeys, and also a determined attempt to introduce parkland and 'green' areas in the city through fingers of open land and landscaping and tree planting. Some of these green zones are termed 'functional orientation areas'. Whatever they call them, they are giving the city green lungs, making life more pleasant for everyone.

Alleyway, central Shanghai   Teenage Fashionistas, Shanghai

Interestingly, the Garden City Movement, which originated in the UK, is celebrated in the exhibition, as a successful pioneer of new towns worldwide, and there are black and white photographs of Welwyn Garden City as it initially looked like just after the Second World War. Another British connection which is celebrated here is the Shanghai Metro. This owes its origins to an electric tram system which was introduced by a British company in the second half of the nineteenth century. We are informed that the Shanghai Metro currently has 15 lines, 331 stations, and in 2016 it carried 6.24 million passengers. These statistics look impressive to me.

On our way back to the hotel, our wheelchair route is blocked by a floral display, spilling out, as it were, from a shop and across the entire width of the pavement. My way back from the pavement onto the road is barred by several parked scooters. At this point I take the law into my own hands. I attempt to remove two of these floral creations to clear a pathway for Sylvia's wheelchair, but they come crashing to the ground. As I attempt to reposition them as best I can, I am aware of a young woman on the opposite side of the road taking photographs of me wreaking havoc, and she seems amused.

An hour later, walking past the same spot, I notice that the gap I created is still there. During the previous hour I have gone out for a walk on my own, along some of the side streets or alleyways off Fuzhou Road. There are lots of small shops at ground level, many of which are beauty parlours, some of them selling wigs. Several mews-style courtyards run off these streets, which are congested back alleys and places for social interaction (lots of it going on); these are villages within the city. The buildings, averaging 3-4 storeys high, are part of the fabric of the city as it was a century ago, despite the additions of neon signs and satellite dishes.

Shanghai Customs House and City Hall

Huangpu River, Shanghai

Around four o'clock, in gently falling rain, Sylvia and I push eastwards from our hotel towards the main promenading area and social hub of Shanghai, known as The Bund. We pass at least half a dozen neighbouring bookshops, possibly the greatest concentration in China. As its name implies, The Bund is a huge revetment, albeit glorified and beautified with hard and soft landscaping and popular walkways, which controls the course of the Huangpu River where it flows through the city centre. Even in the half mist and light rain, this place has an iconic feel about it, as we cast our eyes across the river to a number of skyscrapers, their peaks still shrouded in mist, which if anything, adds to the atmosphere.

Once onto The Bund, which involves Sylvia having to climb, with me pulling the wheelchair up two flights of steps, one of the most famous sights in the world comes into view; the majestic sweep of the river with traditional buildings behind The Bund, and the line of impressive skyscrapers on the opposite bank. We pass several moored boats, one connected with the immigration service and another used by the marine police. Eventually, when we are starting to think that all hope of finding a river cruise is lost, I spot a sign, directing us down a steep ramp, where firm wheelchair control is needed if Sylvia is going to arrive in one piece. A lady directs us to the ticket office, after which we get priority access onto the boat. We choose a window table to sit at and watch the world go by.

Shortly afterwards the boat fills up completely and it moves away from the quayside and into the flow of the river. A young lady approaches us and asks if she can sit with us on our table, as spare seats are now at a premium. Her name is Jessica (or at least this is her English name). She says she is an interior designer, with a specialism for encouraging people to maximise the space in their home. She lives in Donguan city with her husband and little girl and she has arrived in Shanghai for a conference to do with her work. I have no idea how far her home is from Shanghai, but she says she took a flight to get here. Like us, it's the first time Jessica has visited Shanghai and she is enjoying the boat ride and briefly leading the life of a tourist.

Two ladies squeeze themselves into the space just behind our chairs, where they are wedged in by a wall. They are a mother and her 18 year old daughter, who in my view could pass as sisters. They are very keen to have photographs of us taken with them. They tell me, with Jessica doing an admirable job as an interpreter, that I look young, but young in comparison to what I wonder? I think they are doing their best to be polite.

The Huangpu River must be about twice the width of the Thames as it flows through central London at Westminster, and there is plenty of commercial traffic, including large, ocean going vessels, plying the waters. Some of the traditional nineteenth century buildings to our left are set out in graceful, classical proportions, aligned in a curve, which is defined by The Bund. The sublime structure of the City Hall in particular displays slender Greek columns and it must have made a powerful statement about the importance of the city based on world trade about a century ago.

After an hour or so, our boat turns around in the river, and we catch direct views of the office towers, the highest landmarks in the city, on the far bank.

The Bund, Shanghai

As dusk progresses, Shanghai's skyscrapers are transformed by laser lights, with many of the images moving and changing colour, forming a dynamic backdrop to the river. Several of the pleasure boats are also colourfully illuminated, contrasting with the constant flow of the grey, industrial barges and larger ocean going vessels plying their commercial routes, regardless of the colour and celebration of the activities around them. Even in the damp conditions, the illumination of the waterside buildings, from the classical to the futuristic, is gloriously atmospheric. When it seems as if it can't get any more impressive, Jessica notices a wedding party on board a vessel and almost immediately a great cloud of balloons is released over the river.

We invite Jessica back to our hotel for an evening meal with us and she is happy to accept. So the three of us alight from our cruising boat and make our way from The Bund, up a rain-

Shanghai waterfront

sodden Fuzhou Road, with the wheelchair having its work cut out negotiating its way past a lot of street furniture, not to mention the irregular variations in the pedestrian pavements.

Over dinner, we get to know Jessica a little more. She says her husband wants her to join him as a business partner; apparently he sells a range of products via Amazon, and their business plan for the enterprise aims to break even by the end of year two. Jessica seems happy to help him in his entrepreneurial venture. It all sounds quite exciting to me. She also seems to have a great relationship with her four year old daughter. She says they count in Spanish every day, which strikes me as being a fun thing to do with a four year old.

We talk a fair bit over our meal about language, and Jessica says she practises English for 20 minutes every day, which strikes me as being dedicated. The official book that her course is based on is CS Lewis' *The Magician's Nephew*. Jessica is surprised that we have heard of this author, and even more surprised when Sylvia rattles off the titles of all the seven books in the Narnia series (which starts with the *Magician's Nephew*). She also doesn't know that CS Lewis wrote science fiction (after a fashion) and theology.

At around a quarter past nine, we exchange e-mail addresses and hugs before she catches a taxi for her hotel near the airport. Her work-based meeting starts tomorrow at 08:00 hrs and I almost feel guilty thinking that unlike her, we are going to have a fun day looking around Shanghai. Jessica says she would like to visit us in England; that would be great and we look forward to it.

Before going to bed, I start reading John Grisham's *Camino Road*.

Jessica and Sylvia on The Bund

Sunday 20 May 2018

Old Shanghai

We both experience a bad night; Sylvia in particular has found it hard to sleep, which means I did. At 09:30 we are collected from our hotel by Grace, our tour guide, together with our designated wheelchair pusher, who goes by the name of Mrs Su. Mrs Su is a traditional looking lady, maybe in her forties, with no English but she has a happy smile, and as we are about to discover, she has a dogged determination.

Old Shanghai   Yu Gardens

The rain is slight, but it is verging on being cold for the first time on our visit to China. We make it onto The Bund and then walk past a number of buildings dating from the 1920s, including the old Customs House and the former City Hall, dating from a time when Shanghai was extending its world horizons. The former Japanese Navigational Building sells diamonds now. Although the civic and commercial functions of many of these fine buildings have been lost, their elegance and historic importance remains.

Back in the people carrier, we progress further along the river bank, past The Bund, to the Old Town, where the three-storey houses and tenements are packed close together, and many facilities are shared. Within this area we come across the traditional Yu Gardens, said to be 450 years old and which are enclosed by buildings with traditional upturned eaves. Our guide says that the restaurants are squeezed so close together that in former days, it was possible to use your chopsticks to take food from the neighbour's table!

Sylvia spots a jewellery shop and buys a silver chain. A traditional tea ceremony is taking place upstairs on the same premises. Then we pass through a gate leading into the walled gardens of the Yu Gardens complex, at a point where the VIPs of the merchant class used to meet inside a mahogany lined room. The symbols in the room portray wealth and longevity, pointing to a mystic 'double happiness'.

Carp, some of considerable proportions, fill the pool next to the merchants' gate. They are accompanied by a few turtles. Next to the impressive rockery, there is a zig-zag bridge, designed apparently in accordance with 'feng-shui' principles, to keep the evil spirits away.

A leafy road in the French Concession, Shanghai

Dr Sun Yat Sen's house in the French Concession

Leaving the Yu Gardens complex, we come across rows of empty old houses awaiting demolition, with no evidence of any intervention for refurbishment. Some of Shanghai's nineteenth and early twentieth century heritage is being lost and no one seems to care. These older properties are located cheek by jowl with luxury apartments or condos with names such as 'Sun Wonderland'. Some of these condos have grandiose entrances with golden statues, colonnades and even water features.

We walk into a nearby retail store where we find a restaurant on level two. Grace says the Chinese will eat anything with four legs, except tables and chairs! She has to be our guide with the most developed sense of humour!

A short drive later, our driver deposits us in another historic part of the city known as the French Concession. The French, British and Americans, in what for all intents and purposes, were colonial powers in China at the time, were each allocated an area in the city for residential purposes in the interests of foreign trade. In reality, in the early part of the twentieth century, the authorities in Shanghai had little choice but to accede to these neo-colonial demands from the world powers at the time.

Marriage Market, People's Park, Shanghai

Zhou Zhang – water village

The French Concession is perhaps the most distinctive of these areas, with estates of whitewashed villas and substantial tree cover. There are a couple of leafy squares and a lot of the architecture is reminiscent of the French Quarter in New Orleans. Although the area is not free of traffic, there is a calmer, more relaxed feel here than in much of the bustling city which surrounds this inlier of tranquillity. I ask Grace to stop at the former home of Dr Sun Yat Sen, who is recognised by many as the father of modern China, which is quite an accolade. It is clear that he once lived in a well-proportioned villa-style house within the French Concession.

Grace is keen to show us the building where the first meeting of the Chinese Communist Party took place in 1921. It is now a museum. What is remarkable is that this historic meeting took place in what is sometimes referred to as the colonial era when the country was overrun by war lords. This was a time when concessions were granted to the US, France and the UK, foreign powers taking over sections of the city. In the museum, there is a picture of Mao Zedong as a young man. The meeting in 1921 took place right under the noses of the colonial powers, which held sway in the capitalist world of the time, but who little realised what would happen in a matter of decades to the very fabric of China.

After our guided tour, Sylvia rests up in the hotel for a few hours. I 'go it alone' and take a walk into People's Square. Even in damp weather, the square is very popular on this Sunday afternoon. I notice a concentration of umbrellas, and it looks like they are for sale. Each one has messages pinned on top, and there seems to be a fair amount of wheeling and dealing going on. Apparently what I am observing (so Grace informs me later) is a marriage market, with each umbrella providing details of a prospective marriage partner, who for the present is a child, but who is in the process of being married off a decade or two down the line. This is not ours to reason why...

En route to the hotel I drop into the Raffles shopping complex, a huge mall on seven levels, including a mega sized gym on the top floor. This is a favourite place for young couples; romantic clinches on the down elevators at level four seem to be à la mode.

I spot a pizza parlour on the third floor and book a table for two for seven o'clock this evening. The weather outside is dry but humid and my rain jacket is starting to cling, so I take it off and carry it back to the hotel. I rest up for a couple of hours before Sylvia and I set out for our non-Chinese evening meal.

I wheel Sylvia down to the Raffles centre in light rain. In the main mall, I struggle to find a lift to take us to the third floor, and just when I think no-one has the foggiest idea what I want, a lady cleaner gesticulates for us to follow her. She takes us down a narrow passage, turns a corner – and hey presto! There is a lift which takes us up to level 3. I'm not sure that we would have found the lift on our own.

The lady on reception at the pizza parlour remembers me from a few hours ago and leads us to a table. Although we have really enjoyed the authentic Chinese food on our travels for the past three weeks, I can't remember the last time I enjoyed a pizza so much. Even more amazingly, Sylvia is too full even to consider ordering a tiramisu for dessert!

It's relatively quiet and peaceful in the restaurant as we enjoy our pizzas. There's a minor scuffle on the table immediately behind Sylvia, when the boyfriend snatches his girlfriend's mobile phone, and then she snatches his. But it doesn't get any more exciting than that. By the time we have finished our pizzas, the rain has stopped, but it is still quite cold.

Back in our hotel, we share a lift with three guys who have clearly had a lot to drink. One of them presses the wrong button, and then turns and says something to me in Mandarin, which I guess must be an apology. I use one of the very few Mandarin expressions I know – "*Mei guanshi*" (no problem) and the three guys find this very funny; maybe the source of the humour is that they find my pronunciation of the Mandarin is appalling, but I will never know.

I read a little bit more Grisham and it's an early night.

Monday 21 May

The Water Village

We drive for one and a half hours through the rain to Zhou Zhaung, which is a water village, situated near the Grand Canal which runs between Beijing and Shanghai, dating from the Qing Dynasty.

Our people carrier leaves Shanghai via an elevated highway, which Grace tells us can only be used by locally registered vehicles. *"What happens to unauthorised users?"* I ask. *"Seriously punishment!"* says Grace, maybe a bit too gleefully. Apparently, non-Shanghai registered cars have to slum it on a lower level, on a congested highway. The highway we are driving along is a bit like driving on an elevated version of the M6 Toll motorway back in the UK, although with the M6 Toll, everyone can drive on it but most drivers, on principle, don't.

| Canal, water village | Wine distillery, water village |

Electronic traffic boards reveal the extent of traffic congestion on several stretches of the highway and junctions ahead, including nearby, alternative roads, ranging from green, which gives the all-clear, to yellow indicating congestion, and red to highlight gridlock. It looks impressive to me.

Artisan, water village

Waitresses at the Pigs' Trotters Restaurant, water village

Grace then comes out with a joke – *"why do the French like eating snails?"* Answer – *"because they don't like eating fast food..."*

(Boom, boom!) I tell her I think it's quite a good joke, but then I'm not French.

We drive across a low lying area of wetlands and at one point the road crosses a huge fresh water lake – Dian Shan Lake – on a long bridge. We cross several more waterways, some being used by commercial traffic, which cut across this flat landscape.

Despite the weather forecast, the rain stops by the time we arrive at Zhou Zhaung. The water village, as its name implies, is located on a number of canals which criss-cross each other, forming a watery lattice. Most of the tracks and alleyways are car-free. However, describing it as a peaceful place would be wide of the mark. A lot of people, mostly tourists, cram into the narrow alleyways which are a little wider than the average canal towpath back in the UK. Some of the tourist group leaders and guides bark out instructions over loud speakers, which I find quite overwhelming in the narrow confines of these pedestrian routes.

Grace, our guide, Mrs Su, our pusher, and Sylvia, at the water village

We visit a nobleman's house, at least two hundred years old we are informed, with one reception area for the nobleman and another one for his wife. Hers is smaller than his, with a lower roof, reflecting her secondary status in traditional Chinese society. Their small garden is secluded and it adjoins a small water channel enabling him to use the main canal with his boat; great for rapid commuting in the Qing dynasty. The garden also houses a small Buddhist temple, presumably just for family use. A large sheet of marble hangs in one of the rooms (I've no idea of its purpose) in what is a labyrinthine building.

Back on the footpath, there is a lot of pushing and shoving, which is inevitable with so many people negotiating these confined spaces. Someone brushes past me with a T shirt which reads: "*Never trust a man who doesn't like cats*". I'm sure there is a hidden meaning there somewhere.

We find a small shop selling traditional Chinese music on CDs, and we make the shopkeeper work very hard before choosing a few from his extensive collection to take home to the UK. There is a wide range of traditional shops and outlets, including clothing made on ancient hand looms and a rice wine distillery. Cottage based industry appears to be thriving in this interesting place.

Mrs Su, our intrepid wheelchair pusher, manages to steer Sylvia purposefully through the heavy human traffic. It's not only the crowds, but the uneven flagstones which make pushing a wheelchair something akin to negotiating an obstacle course. But Mrs Su sticks to Sylvia's wheelchair like glue. At one point she says something to Grace in Chinese, which Grace then translates and says to Sylvia: "*Mrs Su says that Mike is good with the wheelchair – he is very considerate*"... Sylvia agrees.

We stop at a canal-side restaurant where the local delicacy is pigs' trotters; the story apparently goes back 600 years to a rich businessman who was a friend of the emperor and he was rewarded with a herd of pigs, doubtless of imperial pedigree. And it's been pigs' trotters on the menu ever since. A friendly young woman serves us and she has a lovely smile; which of course is a cue for a photograph, although I take a picture of her together with her two colleagues so as to make her feel less self-conscious.

One of the highlights of the day is on the return journey to Shanghai when our driver swerves to prevent the car from hitting a goat! And he does it with aplomb.

We end the day back in Shanghai with a final walk along Fuzhou Road to the pizza parlour we visited yesterday, just off People's Square; the lure of European cooking, late on into our holiday in China, is becoming irresistible! After a relaxing meal, everyone we encounter on our way back to the hotel is very helpful, such as opening doors for us; one guy even asks in English if we need any help when I manoeuvre the wheelchair up a kerb. People have been kind to us in Shanghai.

Rice fields near Chengdu

Tuesday 22 May

Back to the UK

All our Wendy Woo guides have presented us with a questionnaire for us to comment on how well (or otherwise) they have done and what our experiences have been like. Grace's forms which she gives us to complete are more detailed than all the others put together. But, filling in forms aside, we have been impressed with the personal attention, including awareness of disability, that we have experienced with our Wendy Woo tours and we would certainly use them again.

We depart from our hotel at half past seven in the morning. The city traffic is light at this relatively early hour as we drive along The Bund for the last time. It's a misty morning; the skyscrapers are buried in low cloud as we head towards the tall and graceful Nangpu Bridge. Once over the river, we pass serried ranks of high-rise apartments. The maglev station appears on our right. The maglev is a revolutionary form of travel. The trains ride on a cushion of air, reaching speeds of up to 430 kph; there isn't the distance between the city centre and the airport, however, for the trains to reach their maximum design speed of 540 kph. I keep a close lookout for any maglev trains in between helping Sylvia with putting on her flight socks in the back of the car.

After about 45 minutes, the high rise apartment blocks give way to much lower rise residential development (3-4 storeys) and more trees; this resembles leafy suburbia from our elevated highway.

The well landscaped approach to Shanghai International Airport gives us the feel of driving through a garden, whilst the gleaming new architecture of Terminal 2 is impressive – it's a steel and glass structure with a wavy roof, positively celebrating air travel.

Grace helps us through the procedures until we hit security, at which point we say *"goodbye"*, or as Grace puts it, *"until next time"*. Let's hope so.

Apart from a 40 minute delay in taking off, we enjoy a smooth flight back to the UK. We touch down at London Heathrow Airport safely, with excellent access staff, who are so pleasant and professional.

And the Grisham, which I eventually finish on the train back from London to the West Country, is a good read.

The Gang of Four at Xian